miss new york has everything

"With her refreshingly down-to-earth stories from a high-flying life, Lori Jakiela takes readers on an interesting and engaging trip. Wry and insightful, Jakiela makes a wonderful guide, making the foreign feel familiar, and the familiar, funny. Enjoy the trip."

—Jennifer Traig, author of *Devil in the Details*

"Vividly written, Ms. Jakiela's bittersweet memoir is for every daughter who sees in her father what no one else can see. The kind of love that knows his faults and loves him even more in spite of them."

—Adena Halpern, *Marie Claire*'s "The Haute Life" columnist and author of *Target Underwear and a Vera Wang Gown*

"Funny and provocative ... In MISS NEW YORK HAS EVERY-THING, we observe suburban Pittsburgh in the rare and precious way it once was, with Lauren Tewes of *The Love Boat* fame and horror king George Romero (*Dawn of the Dead*) as symbolic characters and Marlo Thomas as the *That Girl* to which everyone aspires. Jakiela's prose is clean and spare, infused with energy."

—Lee Gutkind, editor of *Creative Nonfiction* and award-winning author

"A quick, engaging pop culture journey through the surprising worlds of amateur beauty pageants, rock-and-roll dating, and starving flight attendants who hate to fly, MISS NEW YORK HAS EVERYTHING manages to be honest, moving, and laugh-out-loud funny all at once. This is the real *Sex and the City* . . . A great debut."

—Dinty W. Moore, author of *The Accidental Buddhist*

more . . .

"A remarkable debut . . . Jakiela's twisting dioramas, voices, and out-rages tell a Rabelaisian and postfeminist tale, to be sure. They also haunt us while we dream our own dreams of insatiable wandering and thirst. A page-turner and a lasting gift."

—Judith Vollmer, award-winning poet and author of *Reactor, The Door Open to the Fire*, and *Level Green*

"Jakiela's memoir is filled with hilarious stories about how she traded in the pill-popping nuns, horny Santas, and ferocious poodles of her small-time town for the wider range of absurdities she encounters as a flight attendant. Underlying the humor is the poignant story of a family of cynical romantics and disillusioned dreamers—some wandering and some stuck in place, but all endlessly questing for home."

—Rachel Manija Brown, author of *All the Fishes Come Home to Roost: An American Misfit in India*

"Told in gemlike chapters, Lori Jakiela's story takes flight both metaphorically and emotionally as it reveals her dreams, her heart-break, and her courage."

—Jonathan Ames, author of *Wake Up, Sir!*

"Heartbreakingly funny, painfully perceptive, and one heck of an engaging read . . . embodies the bittersweet paradox that although you can't escape where you come from, you can always go home again."

—Jen Lancaster, author of *Bitter Is the New Black*

"Jakiela's story of leaving a small town in western Pennsylvania for the glamour of New York and a flight attendant's job is a classic American tale, but one that reads like Hemingway channeling the Marx Brothers. It's the best memoir I've read in years."

—Ed Ochester, author of *The Land of Cockaigne* and *Snow White Horses: Selected Poems*

miss new york has everything

Lori Jakiela

NEW YORK   BOSTON

Some of the chapters in this book have previously appeared, often in other forms, in magazines and newspapers, including *Double Take, River Styx, Brevity, Nerve Cowboy, In Pittsburgh,* and *Pittsburgh City Paper*.

The events in this book are true. Some names and identifying characteristics have been changed.

5 Spot

Warner Books
Time Warner Book Group
1271 Avenue of the Americas, New York, NY 10020
Visit our Web site at www.5-spot.com.

5 Spot and the 5 Spot logo are trademarks of Time Warner Book Group Inc.

Printed in the United States of America

First Edition: January 2006
10 9 8 7 6 5 4 3 2 1

Library of Congress Cataloging-in-Publication Data

Jakiela, Lori.
    Miss New York has everything / Lori Jakiela.— 1st ed.
       p. cm.
    ISBN 0-446-69553-X
    PS3610.A566M57 2006
    813'.6—dc22

                                                      2005022142

Book design and text composition by Nancy Singer Olaguera,
   ISPN Publishing Services
Cover design by Brigid Pearson and Tricia Reinhold

For Dave Newman,
for Carol at 30,000 feet,
and for my father, who loved to fly

acknowledgments

The author owes eternal beers and thanks to the following:

Dave Newman, my outrageous husband, who kept the light shining; who bullied, cajoled, encouraged, and comforted; who was a relentless editor and an open-all-night reader; who juggled the kids and kept a galaxy of worlds spinning; who put his own writing on hold and gave me the impossible gift of time. Thank you for this lucky, lucky life. I love you.

Everyone in the Pittsburgh writing community, especially Ed Ochester, who taught me how to praise; Judy Vollmer, my home girl and soul sister; the ubiquitous Dave Newman; the always spicy Bob Pajich; Jeff Martin, for taking the time to read this book in manuscript; Brian Estadt; Chuck Kinder; Marty Levine, Chris Potter, Heather Mull, and all the folks at *Pittsburgh City Paper*; Betsy Ochester; Britt Ochester and Spring Church Books; Ned Ochester; Adam Matcho; and many, many more.

My agent, Laurie Abkemeier, who fearlessly took me on despite my very perky phone voice. Without your constant prodding and cheerleading, your brilliant editorial comments, your record-breaking ability to endure authorial whining, this book or I would never have made it out of my basement. In short, you rock. Oh yes you do!

Brian DeFiore and Kate Garrick from DeFiore and Company; my smart, hip, and luminous editor, Amy Einhorn, and her assistants, Jim Schiff and Emily Griffin, and everyone at Warner Books; all the other editors who've endured me over the years, especially Joe Shields and Jerry Hagins at *Nerve Cowboy*, Richard Newman at *River Styx*, and David Caddy at *Tears in the Fence*.

Trish Reinhold, the best damn artist and friend ever; Mike Allshouse, my life brother, without whom no Newmans or Jakielas would be left standing; the great literary legend Gerald Locklin, whose writing is matched only by his good heart; and the eponymous Dinty Moore, to whom I owe eternal beers plus two.

All the New York flight attendants—the bravest and sweetest people ever to float above this planet—especially Carol Agostinelli, Super-Tammy Knopf, Carrie Wagner, and Kim Howard.

Paula Leuzzi, who taught me how to handle a rinse cycle; Ann and Frank Kearns; Sinead Lawless; Lou Katz; Ghislain Rykebusch; Margie Vinkler; the ever-cool Rich Blevins and everyone in the writing program at the University of Pittsburgh at Greensburg, Norm Scanlon, and, most especially, my students.

The good people of Trafford, Pennsylvania, who've taught me how to go on living. And finally, Locklin and Phelan Newman—the most powerful super-duo ever; and, in memory, my parents, who taught me how and why to dream.

contents

i am not a zombie, but i played one on tv

"These are simple people. They have little, but
they do not give it up easily. The dead, they give up
to no one."
  —Priest in the basement, *Dawn of the Dead*

"You underestimate these suckers and
you get eaten."
  —Peter in the basement, *Dawn of the Dead*

Rick Krasinski believed he was going to be famous.

This was the winter of 1978. Krasinski, a pimply-faced
brute who smelled like pot and cabbage and wore the same
AC/DC HIGHWAY TO HELL T-shirt for days and snapped my
training bra, puffed and hacked and pretended to spit loo-
gies in my hair, actually spit in my hair, and otherwise ter-

rorized me every second of my eighth-grade year from his designated seat in the back of the Penn Trafford bus, had just gotten a movie deal.

That's what he called it. A movie deal.

One day, on the way home from school, he stood up and shouted, "Hey all you retards. I got a movie deal. I'm going to be a star. I'm not riding this freakin' bus anymore, retards. What do you think about that?"

And it was true. The next day, and the next, Krasinski's seat was empty. The window next to his seat was free of graffitied penises and the gratuitous FUCK FUCKING FUCK. My long hair stayed loogie-free. My back was welt-free. The bus driver was happy. I was happy. We were all—all of us retards—happy.

None of us knew much about movie deals, but everyone knew that director George Romero was in town, filming *Dawn of the Dead* at the Monroeville Mall, our local mecca, home of Orange Julius, The Piercing Pagoda, and the greatest indoor ice-skating rink in Allegheny County. For months, there had been ads in the *Pennysaver*'s Careers section. A movie production company was looking for extras, filming on location in Monroeville and Pittsburgh, open casting calls, show up at 6 AM in the Monroeville Mall parking lot.

All of Trafford had been buzzing with the news. Trafford, Pennsylvania—population 3,002. Trafford, Pennsylvania—home of the Win-Big Bingo and two dueling family-run funeral homes that handed out matchbooks with slogans like DON'T GO WITHOUT US and WE GIVE YOU PEACE OF MIND UNTIL YOU REST IN PEACE.

Shortly before Romero arrived, Westinghouse—Trafford's main employer—suddenly closed its plant, leaving behind toxic waste that would take the EPA decades to clean up. My dad, a machinist, had been lucky—he'd left the big mills years before and already had a job he hated at a small tool company in a town called Wall. He specialized in graphite and came home most days looking like a coal miner or Al Jolson in blackface. As for the other families in the neighborhood, the Westinghouse unemployment lines kept them stocked with government butter and cheese.

Named for Old Trafford, near Manchester, England—home of Rod Stewart's favorite soccer team, the great Manchester United—this new Trafford didn't offer much New World hope. And so, when Hollywood came to town, many of us, like Krasinski, sprouted dreams.

And why not?

After all, 1978 was turning out to be Trafford's year.

Take Lauren Tewes, for example. Born in 1954 in Trafford, the third of four children, Tewes—pronounced, she said, like "tweeze your eyebrows"—had just been cast as Julie McCoy, the perky and charming cruise director on the new hit TV show *The Love Boat*.

Sure, Tewes's family left town when she was eight and has been living in California ever since, and Tewes herself rarely mentions her hometown in interviews, and she was dismissed from *The Love Boat* in 1984, reportedly because of a nasty coke habit and her tendency to chunk up. But ask anyone in Trafford back in 1978 and they'd tell you that *TV Guide* called her a young Grace Kelly, the next Kate Hepburn, Mary Tyler Moore.

Tewes's co-star, Fred Grandy, who played Gopher, put it this way: "Cast badly, her character could make you sick to your stomach. Lauren doesn't make you sick."

And so when Rich Krasinski stopped showing up on the bus, we had reason to believe that, even though he was a bastard and his face was mostly one big pustule, he might just have made it after all.

The local newspapers would run stories about the filming, and I followed them, always checking to see if Krasinski's name would show up. It didn't. There were, however, stories about Tom Savini, a Pittsburgh native and special-effects professional, whose recipe for blood—a sticky fluorescent blend of food coloring, peanut butter, and cane sugar syrup—once ran in the Food section of the *Pittsburgh Press*.

Because of the film's low $1.5 million budget, Savini, when he wasn't creating explodable heads or gnawable thigh bones, doubled as a zombie and as one of the film's two stuntmen. One shoot called for Savini to tumble over the mall's second-floor railing. He did, and just missed the pile of cardboard boxes that would have cushioned his fall. He hurt his legs and back, and for a week or so kept working from a golf cart.

"Miss work?" Savini said. "The director would eat me alive."

Romero, as it turns out, did make a convincing zombie—he played the Santa Claus Biker Zombie in the film.

All of the zombies were, in fact, so convincing, the production company had to take out insurance.

"Say some little old lady sees a zombie walking through the mall the morning after filming," Romero said. "We had to be insured for any harm she might suffer from the shock."

Nothing could compensate for the shock when, the week after Christmas break, Krasinski was back in his seat on the bus, giving the finger to a gaggle of Smurf-lunch-box-toting first-graders waiting with their mothers at the bus stop.

"Some crock of shit," he said so that everyone on the bus could hear. "Three weeks off, Christmas fucking shopping season. Ho ho ho. I said, screw this. They weren't going to jerk me around, the jagoffs. Besides, I knew you all missed me."

Krasinski's movie-deal contract turned out to be a release all extras had to sign. Extras were paid twenty dollars and a box lunch. They got a DAWN OF THE DEAD T-shirt. Krasinski wore his T-shirt, which was two sizes too small, every day for a week. Then he went back to AC/DC.

I almost felt sorry for him. But then he started bringing Savini's blood-blend on the bus and one day smeared it on my butt in one big handprint.

When *Dawn of the Dead* came out the following year, I went to see it, even though I hate horror movies. I watched most of it through my fingers, trying to spot Krasinski in the crowd of blood-spattered flesh-eating fiends.

Every one looked like everyone.

He fit right in.

seasons in the sun

Back in the 1970s, when I was learning how to smoke cigarettes and tie a slip knot as a member of Girl Scout Troop
18 in a church basement in Trafford, Pennsylvania, I had
heard of Jacques Brel.

"It's Jacques *Brel*," I said, pushing the words up over
my tongue and through my nostrils in what I hoped was
authentic French. I was talking to my friend Tricia Fusinelli,
the resident impresario of Troop 18 and my partner for that
year's Trafford Youth Talent Show. "Not Jacques *Prell*.
He's French. He's a singer. He's not a shampoo."

I was making what I thought was a solid argument for
"Seasons in the Sun," a Jacques Brel piece made famous in
the States first by the Kingston Trio, then by two-hit wonder Terry Jacks.

Good-bye to you, my trusted friend.

That Jacques Brel.

I grew up in the years before America had Freedom
Fries. I didn't know much about Brussels or Paris, but I
believed in them the way some people wished on stars.
These were beautiful exotic places filled with beautiful

exotic people, as far away from rat-trap Trafford as you could get.

I watched Jacques Cousteau's TV specials, and believed that Cousteau, with his big nose and wonderful accent, could really ask a dolphin what it had for lunch. I knew what my parents told me—the French thought they were better than us, but the French ate dogs and thought Jerry Lewis was funny, so what did they know.

Still, I believed I was worldly because I could pronounce *Jacques Brel*. A year after "Seasons in the Sun" made it big in the United States, another song would teach me enough French to ask strange boys if they wanted to sleep with me. I felt smug when those boys didn't know what I'd said, even though I had no idea what I was talking about. And I was proud that I knew Jacques Brel was not only a singer but also an actor, a film director, and, most important, a poet who was loved by everyone in France, Belgium, and beyond.

I'd seen a picture of Brel, and, in my parents' defense, he did look suspiciously like Jerry Lewis. He had wavy black hair, horsey teeth, and heavy-lidded eyes that looked like they might pop. Although I think many women loved him, he was not handsome, at least not in the rose-washed picture on the sheet music for "Seasons in the Sun," which hit number one in 1974 in both the U.S. and the U.K.

As I prepped for the Trafford talent show, I begged my parents to buy the sheet music. I convinced Tricia that we should perform a heartrending prepubescent rendition of the song and that it would be a sure win.

"It's a weeper," I told her. "Who can resist that?"

The song was a particularly poignant choice for me because America's leading sap poet, Rod McKuen, had translated the lyrics from Brel's French to *American Bandstand* English. McKuen was the first living poet I had the misfortune to stumble upon in my early literary days—a secret I've kept for many years. I'd check his poems and songbooks out of the Trafford Public Library to supplement my out-of-date *World Book of Knowledge* encyclopedias and my mother's discarded *Reader's Digest*s. (We were not, my mother would say, a family of readers.)

Already McKuen had been a terrible influence. At ten, I had rainbow-covered notebooks filled with rhyming poems about birds, flowers, kittens, cotton candy, and the sky. I was partial to purple ink and velvet black-light posters of seagulls and the moon. I thought McKuen was tender and deep. I thought he was beautiful, even if he did have bad teeth and a bowl cut and sometimes forced a rhyme or two.

"I'm going to marry that man," I told my Troop 18 friends.

From what I've read, many people in France and Belgium felt the same way about Jacques Brel.

In Brussels, Brel's hometown, you'll find the official Jacques Brel Foundation. More than a fan club, the foundation is the authority on all things Brel. It also sponsors exhibits, like Brel, The Right to Dream, which features a holographic image of Brel smoking a cigarette and singing "Les Bon Bons."

According to the foundation, Jacques Brel always wanted to be famous. "As a child, he invented thousands of journeys for himself, which he swore to himself would one day become reality."

Before he starred in *The Man of La Mancha*, before he stood in for Marlene Dietrich at the Olympia Theatre in Paris, before he sailed yachts and flew airplanes and loved too many women, Jacques Brel was a Cub Scout with the Albert I Troupe in Brussels. His nickname was "The Laughing Seal."

Back in 1974, even more than I wanted to write bad poems in pretty notebooks, I felt my real potential was on stage. I wanted to be a musician. I got my love of music from my father, who, when I was very young, would sing to me on the porch or before I'd go to sleep. He'd sing, "When Irish Eyes Are Smiling." He'd sing, "That's Amore." He'd sing showtunes like "Begin the Beguine" or "Hello, Dolly," wriggling his voice and eyebrows and puckering up like Carol Channing to make me laugh.

My father had a lovely voice, with a kind of Sinatra lounge-lizard edge, even though my father said Sinatra would never have made it out of Jersey if he didn't have mob connections.

"He had a good voice, but he went dirty," my father said. "Even the Kennedys wouldn't have anything to do with him."

When my father sang, there was a trace of an accent, the Polish he'd grown up on and tried hard to lose. Maybe it was the accent, or maybe it was because singing made him happy, but I always thought my father was most himself whenever he sang.

Once, before I was born, he'd won a contest and had the chance to sing on the radio in his hometown, Braddock, Pennsylvania. He even cut a record—a 78, the same kind of record Jacques Brel cut with an accordion band in 1953, which led to his being discovered by a Parisian talent scout.

My father didn't like to talk about it, but my mother says that he believed those few on-air minutes, along with the record that my father either lost or more likely destroyed—because I never saw it—were his big break. His whole family, his whole neighborhood, had tuned in to listen, and for a long time afterward my father was the famous singer on Braddock's Cherry Way. But no agents called, there was no big record deal, and my father went back to work the next day, loading cases and kegs of Iron City Beer onto a truck.

A few years later, there was the war. Then he got married, became a father, and made a living the way most men in Pittsburgh did—in the mills. If you asked my father why he gave up on singing, he'd say, "I grew up and buckled down." He'd say, "This isn't a dream world." He quit drinking around the same time he quit thinking about Broadway, two things I've always thought were sad because of the escapes his abstinence seemed to deny him. But he still sang at home and at church, where he'd really belt it out, and afterward, over coffee and doughnuts, other parishioners would compliment him on his voice.

Once, when he'd been sick and missed church for several weeks, a woman I didn't know came up to my father and said, "Thank God, you're back. That organist, the one with the fat ankles. God help her, that voice. It goes right to my scalp."

In 1953, Jacques Brel worked in his family's cardboard factory outside Brussels. "But he never missed a chance to sing to anyone who showed an interest," the foundation says. That same year, Brel started singing in Brussels clubs, on what I think were the 1950s Belgian equivalents of Open Mike Nights. He took a stage name—"Jacques Berel, The Eccentric." He used this name for six months.

At the world-weary age of eleven, I'd taken my own stage name: Willow, as in Weeping Willow. On stage, Tricia went by the more exotic Tish. I'd taken piano lessons since the third grade, and was, among my Girl Scout troop anyway, thought to be talented, even if I couldn't stay in rhythm without someone beating a hand on the piano bench beside me. Metronomes didn't work, and I couldn't count time. Vibration was the only thing that seemed to help. Thankfully, Becky Capuleto, a milkmaid kind of girl with a great passion for plaid, volunteered to turn pages and beat her sturdy hand on the seat during the talent show.

This is how our duo became a trio. We were, Tish assured us, the next really big thing. We needed a name, and decided on Pyramid because it seemed mystical in that Led Zeppelin/Zoso kind of way, and because a pyramid has three sides and there were three of us. Becky, a bit of a geek, had argued for Hypotenuse because she thought it was catchy and different.

"Hypotenuse makes us sound fat," Tish said.

And so, Pyramid we were.

Our logo was a pink Eye of Isis.

If our clever name and musical skills weren't enough to convince the Trafford Borough Council to hand over first prize, we also had props and Tish's original choreography. She had taken jazz/tap for two years straight, where she'd cultivated some moves and mastered stage presence. "Seasons in the Sun," with all its weepy angst, offered Tish the chance for an Oscar-caliber performance.

"I'm pulling out the stops," Tish said. She liked stage lingo, something she also probably picked up in jazz/tap. "We're going to break some legs."

Since the speaker in the song had known his good friend since they were nine or ten, Tish figured she'd hold up nine, then ten fingers. For the line where the speaker asks his father to pray for him, Tish would bring her hands together and bow her head. She had a bouquet of plastic carnations to illustrate flowers everywhere, and when it came time for wine and song, she would take an imaginary drink and wobble. The climax was reserved for the final chorus. On the word *die*, Tish would lift one hand to her forehead, pretend to faint, and slowly close her eyes.

This last image, all other delicious melodrama aside, is what made "Seasons in the Sun" a chart-topper in the United States and what made it irresistible to Tish, Becky, and me. The song is morbid. Brel's original title was, in fact, "Le Moribond."

In Brel's lyrics, it's clear that the speaker in the song

has murdered his best friend because his best friend slept with the speaker's wife, Françoise. The speaker, awaiting his own execution, threatens Françoise and all her would-be lovers everywhere, even as he says good-bye. "Be careful. I'll be there."

In McKuen's Disney version of the song—chock-full of birds and flowers, pretty girls, and that ultrapoetic sea creature, the starfish—of course the speaker is dying, but the other details—adultery, murder—are a bit murkier. Françoise becomes little Michelle, and Brel's lightly veiled threat is transformed to a wish. The speaker's spirit—all cotton-candy goodness and light—wants to stay alive in his faithful Michelle's memory. Death can't keep him from a romp in the flowers or a swing on the monkey bars. Count him in. He'll be there.

Still, G-rated or not, in both Brel's version and McKuen's, the speaker is dying, and that, we were certain, was the most romantic thing of all.

There are thick woods all around the house where I grew up—perfect for keg parties or spin-the-bottle make-out sessions—but one area of the woods is particularly popular. As far back as I know, as far back as anyone in my neighborhood and family knows, the spot has been called the Shades of Death. All of the woods are deep and dark and green, but this area is the darkest and greenest of all.

The legend says a woman hanged herself there because of unrequited love. The legend varies. Sometimes the woman was found in her nightgown. Sometimes, her wedding gown. Sometimes, she was naked. Sometimes she left

a note. Sometimes the note read, "I did this for love."
Sometimes, there was no note.

My friends and I thought the story was wonderful.
We'd sneak away from our parents and meet in the Shades
of Death and hold séances with the Ouija board I'd won
with my grandmother at a church bingo. The questions we
asked the dead were always the same—Will I fall in love?
What will his name be? How many children will I have?
Will I be happy? How old will I be when I die?

I was sure I could die at any minute. More than that, I
was sure my parents would die suddenly, just drop over,
and for a while I became obsessed with telling them I loved
them because of this.

"Pass the salt, please, I love you." "Can I watch *The
Partridge Family*? I love you."

Once, my father asked me why I kept saying I loved
him, and I said, "I want it to be the last thing you hear
before you die." He wouldn't speak to me for days, and I
realized that what he wanted me to say was *just because I
love you so much.*

My father didn't share my adolescent intrigue when it
came to death. He was, I suppose, afraid of it, because
whenever the subject came up, he'd get angry. He'd say,
"I'm going to live to a hundred." He'd say, "I'm too mean
to die." He'd say, "I'll be here to watch the bastards burn."

None of this would turn out to be true, of course.

In 1974, when doctors in Brussels first found a tumor
on Brel's left lung, Tricia Fusinelli, Becky Capuleto, and I
were wearing stage makeup, huge red circles on our

cheeks, and layers of Max Factor Siren lipstick. We were singing and playing our hearts out in that church basement before a crowd of maybe a hundred people. Tish pulled out the stops, collapsing like a dying flower onstage as we did a fade-out refrain.

We took second place.

First prize went to an uppity long-haired thirteen-year-old guitar player who did a breathy rendition of "Scarborough Fair." She had come onstage barefoot, a fistful of what I suppose was parsley, sage, rosemary, and thyme in one hand and a guitar in the other.

"Don't worry, princess," my father said after the show. "These things are fixed."

swampland

"The best of everything, down to the toilet seats," my father said.

We were outside his dream house, and it was lovely. Earlier, while my father rapped on pipes, my mother and I had gone room to room, taking it all in. The ceilings were high and accented with wood beams. The windows were huge. One wall of the kitchen was taken up by a sliding glass door that opened onto a deck where, one morning, I saw a lizard. The lizard was a foot long, and its green skin gleamed with flecks of gold. The bathrooms were sherbet-colored with deep shell-shaped bathtubs. Outside, a small dock led into a canal. There was a boat launch.

"Maybe we'll join the yacht club," my father said, and he laughed. Laughing wasn't something my father did very often, and it made my mother and me glad to hear it.

The canal was filled with flying fish that hurled themselves out of the water. Their fins reflected rainbows. When it rained, which it did daily, it rained first on one side of the street, then the other. The sun never stopped shining for long.

• • •

The trip down had been a borderline disaster. Our Chrysler didn't have a stereo. It had an AM radio with loose dials and bad reception. This didn't bother my father. Twenty-two hours, Pittsburgh to Florida, without music, was fine. In fact, he liked it. After he botched his dream of becoming the next Sinatra, he never listened to music.

I was fifteen, though, and was sure I'd be the next Stevie Nicks. Music and lacy peasant blouses were everything to me. But thanks to my father, the only sounds I'd hear for an entire day were wheels on pavement and my parents' bickering. It was enough to make me insane.

When we got on the Pennsylvania Turnpike, it was 5 AM.

"Have to get an early start. Rush-hour traffic is a bitch," my father said. "We've got to get where we're going."

He'd stayed up all night, drinking instant coffee and highlighting AAA Trip Tiks. No sleep and too much caffeine left him looking crazy, like a character out of a Kerouac novel, but without the kicks and joy.

Every year we went to Florida. Every year, the entire trip was filled with my father's fury. He hated his job as a machinist at Radform Tool, where his specialty was graphite. He'd come home most days, his skin and clothes stained black as asphalt, and have to use steel wool to get his hands clean before dinner. For this he got two weeks of vacation. He got a box of chocolates for Christmas. He got a death-and-dismemberment policy.

This is why our family trips felt more like ambulance runs than vacations. For my father, they were urgent. We'd take the Chrysler, a 1967 Newport, his prized car, his Florida car. Aside from our vacations and the occasional funeral, the car mostly stayed in the garage, covered by old quilts and bedsheets.

My father, his hands white-knuckled at ten o'clock and one o'clock on the beach-ball-size steering wheel, would shout "Stuff it already, Jesus Christ" whenever my mother, the navigator, would flip through the Trip Tiks. She'd be certain we were going the wrong way, telling him, "Pull over, pull over, we're going the wrong way," even though we went the same way every year. He'd guzzle the coffee she poured from a Thermos and chain-smoke cigarettes while I huddled down in the backseat and tried to sleep off the whole trip.

When I couldn't sleep, I studied the brochures I collected at rest stops. The brochures, with their pictures of dream destinations and fake happy families, always helped me, an only child, survive an entire day in the car with my parents.

I had brochures for every alligator farm on both sides of Alligator Alley.

I had brochures for Weeki Wachee, where divers from the Orient would plunge into a swimming pool laden with shellfish and bring up pearls—complete with certificates of authenticity—which could be set into rings.

Weeki Wachee also had mermaids—*Lifelike sirens of the deep*, the brochures read. In person, the mermaids were real women, girls, really, with their feet and legs squeezed into glittery blue rubber fins. They could hold their breath and smile underwater. Their mascara did not run. That was the mystery, what brand of mascara, how long could they stay under. I ticked off the minutes in my head.

I knew something was up on this trip when my mother reached back and poked me in the ribs.

"Wake up," she said. "Your father is talking to you."

"We didn't tell you before because you can't keep your mouth shut," my father said, eyeballing me in the rearview mirror. "Next thing you know, you'd be blabbing to the neighbors. They'd think we're rich. We're not rich. Not that it's their business, the cockroaches."

My father called everyone cockroaches, except for family members.

Family members got their own names, like Shirley Temple, The Banker, The Meatball, and The Jehovah. The names were cruel and funny and scalpel-sharp.

Shirley Temple, a woman with no discernible talent, spent her entire adult life bemoaning her lost chances at celebrity. The Banker, my father's brother, was one of the few in his family who didn't get stuck working in the mills. The Banker would say things like, "Let me put your money to work for you." He always wore suits and his shoes were spit-shined. His fingernails were always clean and looked manicured.

"He thinks his shit don't stink," my father would say. "Trust me. It stinks."

The Meatball was my mother's brother. He considered himself 100 percent Italian, even though my grandmother was Slovak and my grandfather grew up in an orphanage and didn't care about his ethnic origins. I almost never saw The Meatball without one of his trademark T-shirts: ITALIANS MAKE BETTER LOVERS, KISS ME I'M ITALIAN, KISS THE ITALIAN COOK, RIDE THE ITALIAN STALLION, IF YOU AIN'T ITALIAN FUHGEDDABOUTIT.

When The Jehovah, formerly a devout Catholic, became a Jehovah's Witness after a bad divorce, she gave away shoe boxes full of dashboard Jesuses and plastic crucifixes, started smiling, and stopped celebrating birthdays and holidays. And although she'd show up at Thanksgiving and Christmas dinner because she loved family get-togethers, cranberry salad, and my grandmother's stuffing, she'd try to sneak copies of *The Watchtower* into everyone's coats and talk about how important it was to keep her house looking nice with crocheted toilet-paper cozies and matching hand towels.

"I'm going to live here for eternity, after Jehovah takes away the evildoers on Judgment Day," she'd say.

My impulse was always to defend her. Whatever she believed, she was sweet and kind, softer than most of the other members of our family.

"She seems happy," I'd tell my father.

"Bullshit," he'd say. "Next thing you know, she's selling flowers and dancing around in a bathrobe at the airport. My mother used to chase people like her off our porch with a broom."

At home, my father kept the curtains drawn and the doors triple-locked. He even tried to convince my mother to let him put bars on the windows. In our neighborhood, the worst crime involved kids who set bags of dogshit on fire at Halloween. My mother said it was either her or the bars, so my father gave up. All the years we lived in that house, from the outside it looked like no one was ever home.

Back in the car, my parents had let me in on their secret. They had built this other house, their dream house, in Cape Coral. That was where we were heading instead of Disney World, as I'd hoped.

The Realty brochures described Cape Coral as *virtual paradise—a lot less like the rest of the world*. Later I'd learn that Cape Coral is famous as the place where, back in 1521, the locals killed Ponce de León and other dreamers like him.

"You know who our neighbors are?" my father said. "Henry Ford, that bastard. Thomas Edison, too."

I didn't remind my father that this was 1979 and both men were dead. I didn't mention that maybe the house wouldn't look the way it did in the Realty brochures. Even at fifteen, I tried not to break whatever happiness he could find. We were people with dreams, like Ponce, like nearly everyone we knew. And sometimes this made us gentle with each other, at least where dreams were concerned.

As far as cures went, my father had Florida, The Jehovah had Judgment Day, and I had my music. Just before we'd left on this trip, I'd been in another talent show, this time at Penn Trafford High School. I'd done Jim Croce's "I'll Have to Say I Love You in a Song." My performance was terrible, but it wasn't for lack of planning. I wore a lacy white dress with bell sleeves that fanned out like wings. I sprang six bucks for some plastic-wrapped roses at the 7-Eleven. I'd carefully arranged the roses across the piano. I even closed my eyes as my fingers floated over the keys and my voice cracked into a mike that, despite being anchored to a stand with electrical tape, squealed feedback.

When it was over, I opened my eyes and tossed the roses into the crowd. Then I saw the judges. They were not smiling. Still, my friend Donnie, who pierced his cheek with a safety pin and wore outfits he'd made out of garbage bags, assured me that my performance had been very moving.

"Your heart was fucking bleeding on that stage," Donnie said. "What more do they want? Stupid hicks. Screw them."

Then again, Donnie wept when he heard Sid Vicious sing "My Way."

Like I said, we tended to be gentle with each other.

As the Chrysler hurled down the turnpike, my mother passed the Realty brochures and pictures over her shoulder. The house was a bubblegum-pink stucco number. In the pictures, the Florida sunsets were postcard-perfect, the sun breaking across the sky like an egg.

"We won't be able to plant grass until the exterminators finish up," my mother said. "Fire ants. Every house has them."

I couldn't imagine how my parents had kept the house

a secret. Back in Trafford, we lived in a tiny ranch. There was little privacy. My bedroom was directly across from my parents' room, and my father did not like closed doors. They must have spent months, years, planning the Florida house, whispering under the sheets like kids at a sleepover.

"For Christ's sake, don't tell that fat Shelley," my father was saying. "Her mother will be out there with a goddamn bullhorn."

Shelley, my friend, lived in downtown Trafford. Although downtown Trafford was half a mile from our house, my father considered it urban and trashy. Even in a place like Trafford, there is a line between the haves and have-nots. Shelley's old neighborhood has row houses and sidewalks and bars. This, according to my father and other people with backyards and driveways and lawn trolls, made all the difference.

In Shelley's defense, her neighborhood wasn't trashy and she wasn't fat. She was big-boned and good at volleyball. But Shelley's mother was a notorious gossip who volunteered as a greeter at St. Regis Church. Every Sunday, she'd stand at the door near the holy water and take note of who was and was not present. She commented on people's outfits or, if she hadn't seen someone for a while, she'd say "Nice of you to show up." At home, she was obsessed with *The Young and the Restless* and wore flowered housedresses she'd bought on sale at GeeBee's.

Shelley's house smelled like fried chipped ham and bacon grease, but there was a real jukebox in the basement. The jukebox, all chrome and neon, was loaded with the best 45s, though we seldom played anything other than "Killing Me Softly." We'd crank it up, whip out two hairbrushes that doubled as microphones, and spend our afternoons putting on a show.

Most of the time, Shelley's mother left us alone and Shelley's father wasn't around. He worked at Westinghouse and liked his overtime more than he liked his wife. When it came to the job, Shelley's dad would take all the hours he could get. He'd brag about how he could go without sleep or a bath for days. He liked to show off his hands, which, like my father's hands, were calloused and peppered with chips of steel.

"See these hands?" he'd say. "Hell, Jesus Christ has nothing on me. You could pound a nail right in there and I wouldn't feel a thing."

He liked to talk about how his boss respected him, how he wasn't going to be forgotten at Christmas-bonus time. He had plans to retire early, maybe leave his wife for a fishing boat and a mail-order bride, then end up somewhere in Florida, like my parents.

But when Westinghouse shut down, it shut down. After school, when I went over to Shelley's, there he was, propped in a recliner in the basement, avoiding his wife and monopolizing our jukebox, which he'd bought with his Christmas bonus a few years before. He'd drink Iron City and belt out Louis Armstrong's "It's a Wonderful World."

Sometimes, he'd see us slowly backing up the stairs and yell, "Don't let them kid you." We'd just nod, close the basement door, then head outside to Shelley's porch stoop, where we'd spend the rest of the afternoon seeking life advice from my Ouija board. When it was working, we trusted the Ouija to spell out the names of our future husbands. It could tell us the number of children we'd have. It could tell us whether we'd be rich or famous. But it couldn't give us the answers we needed most—why our parents were so unhappy and how we could avoid becoming just like them.

Back in the car, my father was still at me.

"Your mother and I, we scraped, we saved. We sacrificed. If you go around talking about a house in Florida, people think you're on easy street," he said, then hit the steering wheel for emphasis. "I am not on goddamn easy street."

There was, I already knew, no easy street. My father didn't have rich relatives in Braddock or Poland. He was never badly injured on the job. And although he didn't believe in bad luck, he was lousy at the lottery. He had a shoe box full of losing tickets to prove it.

"Look how close," he'd say, pulling out ticket after ticket. He'd write the day's winning numbers on each one, so he could compare later. "One number off. One number. Can you believe it? What gives? Tell me, what gives?"

Shelley's dad had a solid losing streak going, too, but that didn't stop both of them from getting in line at Blackburn Dairy whenever the lottery jackpot was high. The line usually stretched to the door. If you wanted to buy a gallon of milk in my neighborhood, you'd have to wait twenty minutes, at least.

My father figured that the lottery, like most talent shows, was fixed. Other people thought this, too, so most of them tried to double their odds with bookies.

"Who cares where the money comes from, as long as it comes," my father said whenever anyone asked about his bookie's mob connections.

"Say you hit every week with a nickel in a box," my father would say in bookie lingo. "Now that adds up. And screw the government—we're talking tax-free."

If the bookies didn't work out for the good people of Trafford, there was, finally, bingo. Bingo was the bottom-feeder on the food chain of hope. I knew. I worked as a waitress on bingo nights at the Trafford Polish Club from the time I was twelve until I went to college. My grand-mother, Ethel, ran the kitchen and paid me cash under the table, plus all the fried fish I could eat. It wasn't a horrible job, but the regulars were usually difficult and desperate, and Ethel, my mother's mother, had a grand reputation as a crusher of dreams.

My aunt, the one my father called Shirley Temple, never missed a chance to remind everyone at family gath-erings that, if it weren't for Ethel, she could have been a contender.

"I was going to be a stewardess," she'd say, gazing wistfully up toward the friendly skies. "I was going to travel all over the world. Someone, I'm sure, would have spotted me. Someone would have seen the talent that's in me."

I didn't even see the inside of an airplane until I was

seventeen, and I didn't understand my aunt's dreams. Sure, *stewardess* sounded exotic and exciting, but the idea of being discovered by a Hollywood talent scout while dishing out coffee and peanuts always seemed a little far-fetched. But my aunt didn't see any irony in her dreams, or in the fact that her mother was the one to squash them flat.

"My mother, she wouldn't have it. 'No child of mine is going off gallivanting,' she'd say. So I took a job at G. C. Murphy's. I worked the perfume counter, a very prestigious position. Handsome men would come in all the time and flirt with me. They'd buy me chocolates and potato chips. They'd offer to take me away from it all. I could have been so much more."

My aunt would sigh her well-practiced sigh while my mother, her sister, rolled her eyes.

I was never sure what my aunt's talent was, exactly. She was not a singer or a dancer. She didn't play an instrument. She wasn't a star in the Trafford Community Theater. She didn't even seem to like movies. She did, however, have a lot of faith in her red hair.

Growing up, I didn't think much of Shirley Temple, although years later I'd take up her dream and become a flight attendant whose ambitions didn't quite fit her uniform. Still, I had to sympathize a little. Where dreams were concerned, Shirley Temple was right. My grandmother didn't take the gentle approach.

Just before the trip to Cape Coral, she'd started up with my father and me.

"I don't know why you people think you have to go

every year," she said. "What are you, the Rockefellers? You're too good to stay home once in a while?"

Ethel was never happy about these annual trips to Florida. We'd taken her with us only once, and she may have been bitter about that. Besides, with me gone for two weeks, she'd be stuck without cheap help on bingo nights. And, like I said, the bingo regulars were tough.

I was the only waitress. On most nights, I didn't get a bathroom break. For two bucks an hour, I'd hustle assorted deep-fried cuisine to a crowd of two hundred or more in this hall where cigarette smoke billowed against the ceiling like Los Angeles smog. The usual tip was a dime, and the customers were so focused on winning and the art of good luck that anything could set them off.

Take the time I bumped Mr. Pisanski's cards. I set down his coffee and touched the corner of one card with the cup. That was it. Bad luck the rest of the night. When someone else would yell bingo, he'd sweep his chips into his hand and make a fist.

"Stupid girl, stupid, stupid girl," he'd say whenever I walked past. "My whole night in the can. Garbage. And all because of you."

And there was Mrs. Buetchner. Mrs. Buetchner was nuts about her good-luck charms. Her troll doll with its fuchsia hair and birthstone belly button went to her left at precisely eleven o'clock. The plastic cow with its rubber udders came next. Lucky dice, sixes on every side, went dead center. Then, on her right, was her lucky rock. This rock had come through Mrs. Buetchner's windshield a few years before. It had barely missed her head as she was driving beneath an overpass on Route 130. She saw this as a sign.

"This rock was sent by God, honey," she'd say, patting my hand and telling me the same story every time she saw me. "God wants me to win."

Then she'd order up some cheeseballs.

I'd like to think divine intervention played a part in my parents' dream house. And maybe my father was, in his own way, blessed. He never ended up like Shelley's dad. He was never laid off. And though his dreams of becoming a famous singer never came true, and he was on a lifelong losing streak with both his bookie and the lottery, and he was a paranoid bingo player who worried too much about other people watching his cards, my father had somehow, miraculously, planned his escape.

"This is the real deal, princess," he said as he flicked a cigarette out the car window and lit a fresh one. "In a few years, if we play our cards right, we'll be la-dee-dah in the sunshine. Screw those Pennsylvania winters. That's no way to live."

A few years before, my father had bought some land in Naples, Florida. He'd responded to an ad he'd seen in *The Liberty Lobby*, a scary right-wing newspaper he subscribed to in the early 1970s. He bought the land without seeing it, figuring we could all check it out during our vacation that year.

I remember a lot about that trip. My father was less furious than usual. He even let me con him into visiting one of the tourist meccas lauded in my rest-stop brochures and featured on more than 250 billboards beginning in New Jersey and arcing down through Florida. South of the Border, or SOB, as insiders call it.

PEDRO SEZ NO SIESTA UNTIL SOUTH OF THE BORDER.

NO MOONKEY BUSINESS, JOOST HANKY PANKY AT SOUTH OF THE BORDER.

PEDRO SEZ ARRIBA ARRIBA TOO MOOCH TEQUILA.

And, especially persuasive for Pennsylvania tourists, EXPLOSIVOS! GET YOUR MEXICAN FIREWORKS AT SOUTH OF THE BORDER.

This particular year—maybe because he was feeling good about the land in Naples, maybe because he wanted to annoy my mother, or maybe because he just wanted me to be happy—my father gave in and we took a detour off I-95 to Dillon, South Carolina.

The ninety-seven-foot statue of Pedro, lit with neon and straddling the entrance, was, to me, the Empire State Building, the Colossus of Rhodes. I made my mother take pictures of me there, between Pedro's legs. In the pictures, I am long and lean, already tan. I'm wearing a puka bead choker, a mood ring that was nearly always black, and a T-shirt emblazoned with a glittery iron-on butterfly. My hands are on my hips and I'm grinning.

I didn't notice anything beyond Pedro's crotch until the flashcubes stopped popping. Then I saw what was missing. There weren't any real Mexicans dozing under glittery sombreros. There were no gorgeous senoritas snapping castanets. Nothing looked the way it did in the brochures.

Here there were only crackling loudspeakers blaring José Feliciano's greatest hits and a musty gift shop stocked with dried alligator heads; tequila-flavored lollipops, complete with worms; and cans of air freshener called EverGlade.

To cheer me up, my father bought me a paperweight. It was a snow globe, really. Inside was the dead and soon-to-be decomposing body of an actual sea horse. The horse bobbed lopsidedly in its snowflake soup. There was a thermometer in there, too, full of real mercury. It read fifty degrees, no matter which state line we crossed.

By the time we hit Naples, the weather was so hot and humid my father worried that the car would simply stop running. I worried about alligators. I scanned the sides of the road and was terrorized by burned-off tire treads. I was sure that my father would be eaten when he finally pulled over and got out of the car. There was nothing around us but a soupy expanse of swamp. The swamp looked like the algae we grew in Mrs. Schullo's science class and smelled like the sulfur creek back home. My father stared for a long time at the piece of swamp in front of him, then at the paper in his hand. My mother stayed with me in the car. When my father came back, no one said anything.

This is what I was thinking—*swampland*—before we pulled into the driveway and saw that the Cape Coral house was exactly what the pictures had promised.

"What did I tell you, princess?" my father said. "I'm a smart man. Nothing gets by me. Is this place something or what?"

It was.

During those two weeks, I felt we were living on a movie set. Everyone was happy. The weather was beautiful. We spent our days going to furniture and specialty stores, buying everything new.

"Only the best," my father said. "We want things to last."

My parents planned to furnish the house and then rent it out for a few years until my father retired. And so we bought everything—silverware, a toaster oven, pots and pans and oven mitts. By the time we were ready to leave, the house looked like a home. We took pictures in every room and my parents held hands.

If I could freeze one moment from my childhood to relive again and again, this would be it. I can't remember any other time when we were all so full of hope.

But then, the next year, we didn't make our annual Florida run. My parents didn't explain. I figured there wasn't much money left after they built and furnished the house. They also had to pay a Realtor to rent it. On top of everything, the tenants weren't working out.

"Cockroaches," my father said. "They want something for nothing."

Then the Trafford house started to run down.

"We need new goddamn gutters, a new roof. The driveway's cracked for Christ's sake. I can't be horsing around. There's work to do," my father said.

The following year, my mother had a heart attack. Her doctors said the heat and humidity in Florida would be dangerous. And so my parents called the Realtor and told her to sell their dream home at a loss. We never saw the house again.

My father never talked about it. When I asked my mother, who in bad times turned to clichés like they were pills, she'd say, "It's in the past. What's done is done."

My parents and I stopped going to Florida after the house was sold. And although they'd continue to travel, even make repeat trips to Europe when I got my airline gig, nothing ever seemed to make them as happy as they were during those few weeks in Cape Coral.

Whenever Shirley Temple would start up at family gatherings, I'd notice my father would leave the room. She'd moved on from her stories of crushed sky-goddess dreams into diatribes about Las Vegas, where she and her husband had become regulars.

"Last time we saw Frank Sinatra at Caesars, I swear he was singing right to me," she'd say. "One of these days, we're just going to pack up and move there. It's paradise. That dry heat. My arthritis doesn't bother me at all. And the buffets! You can't believe the buffets! All the shrimp you can eat. Crab legs, too. They treat you like you're royalty. Like you're somebody."

love your friends,

bite your enemies

We all have something we love beyond reason.

For my father, the steelworker, survivor of the Great Depression and World War II, it was a fluffy white miniature poodle named Tina II.

The use of the word *thing* would have infuriated my father, who insisted that Tina II was more human than any human could ever be, down to the precise number of germs living on her long pink tongue.

"Her mouth is cleaner than ours and that's a scientific fact," he would say as Tina II slathered his face with dog drool. "She can lick her own ass and still be cleaner than any of those cockroaches."

My father used the word *cockroaches* indiscriminately. Usually, however, in a conversation about Tina II, he was referring to the other men who worked with him at Radform Tool. At least once, one of these men had spotted my father in his graphite-smeared work clothes taking Tina II for a walk in our yard. Stories circulated about my father, who had a great reputation as one of the meanest men in the shop, using a spatula and plastic bag to clean up after a poodle who pranced along ahead of him in a red knit sweater and Santa cap.

This story was somewhat embellished. My father tended not to clean up after Tina II, mostly because he didn't want her to feel embarrassed. The sweater was indeed red, though it was crocheted and not knitted. It was the handiwork of my grandmother, who, when she wasn't busy shellacking salt-dough Christmas ornaments or making armies of small soldiers and accordion bands out of thread spools and pipe cleaners, crocheted doggy outerwear for Tina II and her cousin, my aunt Gertrude's poodle, Charm.

Tina II, a particularly fashionable dog, had a collection of sweaters and fringed doggy ponchos with matching hats and little elasticized pouches my grandmother called tail muffs. While she tolerated the sweaters, Tina II hated the muffs and hats, though my mother would try to force them on her anyway. The hat my father's colleague spotted on Tina II would have been one of these everyday tousle caps, and not something Tina II—who once, to preserve what was left of her dignity, had chewed and shredded a green Santa's elf hat down to a moldy hairball—would have worn exclusively for Christmas.

Even though he'd become a punch line at work, my father continued to cater both publicly and privately to Tina II. He did this mostly because, like a lot of his fellow humans, he liked dogs better than people.

"A dog you can trust," my father would say as he

sliced a medium-well steak into dog-size bites or brushed Tina II's ears with a boar-bristle brush he'd bought from an Avon lady exclusively for this purpose. "People are screwballs. With people, you never know."

Andy Rooney, whom my father thought was wise because he made it on *60 Minutes* even though he had those eyebrows and was ugly as sin, once said, "The average dog is a nicer person than the average person."

Years before, Freud had put it this way: "Dogs love their friends and bite their enemies, quite unlike people, who are incapable of pure love and always have to mix love and hate."

My father, although tenderhearted enough to give money to anyone who asked him for it on the street, intensely disliked most people in ways that I suspect surpassed even Freud or Rooney or any other sage who would have thrown down with them in the dog-loving ring. He was probably closest in temperament to the French writer Celine, who could say the word *shit* in seventeen languages and kept company mostly with dogs and whores.

My father's love for dogs was obvious, and I think my father had a soft spot for whores, too, because he once told me a story about how, when his ship landed in Japan during World War II, the streets were full of girls who would trade sex for cigarettes, a shirt, or a pair of shoes. My father gave them his cigarettes, along with some change, and sent them on their way without getting anything in return.

"I hadn't seen a woman in months. I wasn't dead, you

know. But for Christ's sake, these were kids. They were just trying to survive," he said.

My father's kindness and empathy for those strange girls in an enemy land didn't always translate back home, however. Although he was usually sweet to me and mostly tolerated my mother, my father didn't have close friends. He didn't like most of our neighbors. He thought all grocery-store clerks were crooks. He shredded his junk mail long before it was common to do so because he believed the garbagemen were snoops who, according to the conspiracy newspapers he subscribed to, were probably working for the government And although I heard him once say something nice about his bookie and a teller at the bank, the compliment amounted to, "Hey, at least they don't try to screw you on purpose."

I'm not sure where my father's misanthropic tendencies started, but I know they got worse through the years. He'd had a hard life, like most of the people from his generation, but, the story about the whores being one exception, he didn't usually go into much detail with me. Guessing about the nature of his problems never helped me completely understand them. I only knew what I saw. I could watch from my bedroom window when my father was outside with the dog. I could see his lips moving in long, one-sided conversations, and wondered about the things our dog knew about my father that I never would.

If disappointment and heartache were part of my father's problems, Tina II was a constant reminder. It wasn't her fault Tina II was the replacement poodle my parents bought (my father preferred the term *adopted*) when they were devastated by the loss of Tina I. Tina I, a fluffy black miniature poodle who favored haute couture poodle clichés like rhinestone dog collars and pink toenail polish with matching ear bows, had choked to death on a piece of aluminum foil. According to her veterinarian, Tina I had swallowed the foil—actually a chewing-gum wrapper—earlier, but vomited it up during surgery to remove a cancerous teat tumor. The wrapper lodged in her throat, and somehow she suffocated without the vet noticing or doing much about it.

When it suited him—usually if he was losing a fight—my father would blame my mother, an avid chewer of Wrigley's foil-wrapped gum, for Tina I's demise. But he always thought the vet's story was fishy.

"That goddamn vet was a butcher," my father would say. "He didn't know his ass from a hole in the ground. I'd like to operate on him."

When the vet called to tell my parents about Tina I's demise, he said they could pay extra to bury her at the pet cemetery.

"Or I could just take care of it so you wouldn't have to deal with the body," he'd told my mother. "It's easier that way."

"Leech," my father said. "Bloodsucker."

My father went alone to pick up the body. He'd laid Tina I's favorite fuzzy pink blanket in the backseat of the car. I hope that the vet knew enough not to be there when my father arrived, but I never knew exactly what happened at the vet's office. My father wouldn't speak to either my mother or me when he came back home looking weepy and immediately began digging a hole in our backyard near my mother's prized rhododendrons.

Just days after he laid Tina I to rest in her blanket with her squeaky pork chop and one of his tube socks, days after he'd scoured the house looking for stray gum wrappers or bits of aluminum foil as evidence of my mother's guilt and his own innocence, my father packed my mother and me into the car and headed to a local poodle breeder.

There was never a question about whether or not we'd get another dog or which breed that dog would be. Poodles were my family's dog of choice, which was odd, considering we were staunch democrats and my parents eschewed all things French and anything that reeked of aristocracy. My aunt, who for years begged people to call her Trudy instead of Gertrude and hosted Kentucky Derby parties, complete with blenders full of mint juleps and a vat of champagne punch, in her white aluminum-sided house in Turtle Creek, might have felt that Charm added something to her social status. But for my parents, the choice was purely a practical one. Poodles are hypoallergenic and they don't shed. This was important because my father and I had problems with dander and my mother hated to vacuum.

"Poodles aren't even originally from France," my mother would say, having read about it in *Reader's Digest*. "They've been around since Roman times. They were hunting dogs, good swimmers. Then the French took over and made them look like shrubbery."

My parents both believed that the standard topiary-like poodle cut was the cause of all the breed's image troubles.

Whenever my father would see poodles parading around on TV with coiffed dollops of fur bubbled up like inner tubes around their necks and thighs, whenever he'd see Zsa Zsa Gabor mugging for the camera with a custom-dyed pink poodle, whenever he'd see the Drysdales' poodle Claude preening like a celebrity stylist and taunting the old bloodhound on *The Beverly Hillbillies*, my father's reaction would always be the same.

"Rich bitches," he'd say. "Pansies. Ruining a perfectly good dog like that. I'd like to take an electric razor to them. I'd like to dye them pink and see how they like it."

Instead of the traditional poodle cut, our poodles were allowed to go natural. Their fur grew until they looked like sheep. My parents were certain that this was why both dogs had nice, down-to-earth dispositions. Sure, they liked steak, sat on chairs at the dinner table, slept in our beds, and were snappy dressers, but they weren't otherwise snobby. These were working-class poodles, the kind who weren't afraid to chase their own nubbed tails, sniff other dogs' butts, or claw a screen door to get at the mailman who, according to my father, deserved what he got because he did nothing but bring bills.

When it came time to hit the groomers—usually once in the spring, summer, and fall—my parents would leave explicit instructions. Just like sheep, our dogs would come back shorn nearly bare, except for the fur on their ears and one signature pom on their heads and tails. Both Tinas seemed to find this degrading and, upon returning home, would hide behind the sofa or under my parents' bed and try to claw the bows out of their ears with their unfortunately polished front toenails.

I don't remember how we acquired Tina I, but I was around six or seven years old when we went to pick up Tina II. The breeder's house smelled the way you'd expect a house with dozens of dogs in it to smell. The smell of dog was cut only by the breeder's menthol cigarettes, open cans of dog food, and another meat-and-grease smell that I assumed was chili coming from the kitchen, where the floor was covered with newspaper.

When the breeder came to the door, she was restraining a huge gray standard poodle. I'd never seen a standard poodle before. Up until then, I'd thought all poodles were the same size as ours, about the size of a large toaster oven. The standard poodle was closer to the size of a real oven. Plus, it had a poodle cut, with furry bracelets on all four legs and a huge mane. It was, in other words, terrifying. It might as well have been a German shepherd, if it weren't for the pink toenails, the smug epicurean look on its muzzle, and the way it moved like Mrs. Owens, my ballet teacher. Mrs. Owens was originally from Ohio, but she tried to fake a Russian accent to make herself seem more like a defector from the Bolshoi than someone who taught toddlers through preteens pliés at a stair-rail barre in her basement.

I was very frightened of German shepherds, having seen them attack Vietnam protestors on TV and having been cornered by one during a game of hide-and-seek at my friend Jackie Belinski's house a few months before. The memory of Jackie's German shepherd, who kept me pinned against the wall behind Jackie's bed, snarling and breathing its decomposing liver-laced dog-food breath in my face for what seemed like hours and was probably minutes until Jackie's mother came in and called it off, was still fresh. When I looked at this poodle, I expected it to lunge without warning, those black lips and gums pulled back, its eyes blank as a shark's, its teeth the size of steak knives.

"You're lucky," said the breeder, a sort of nondescript middle-aged woman with a teased and lacquered poodle-do. "They're just now ready. You've got your pick."

She held the door open wider and we stepped inside, maneuvering around the standard poodle, who stared at us as if it were a maître d' at a four-star restaurant and we had shown up wearing overalls and without reservations.

In the living room, which was cordoned off with child-safety gates, a litter of adorable poodle puppies chewed each other's ears, stomped on each other's heads, and vied for attention in other ways unbecoming a registered purebred. And these were all registered purebreds, the breeder was quick to tell us.

"I've got papers for all of them," she said. "They'll all make good show dogs."

My father scowled at her. Before he could start, my mother stepped in.

"You go pick, honey. Find a good one now. Remember, we want a girl," she said, opening one of the gates and giving me a shove.

Go figure.

My father was the one most devastated by the loss of Tina I. He was the one with the most invested in developing a good relationship with Tina II. But my parents sent me in to pick our new pet. I'm sure this was a show of great confidence, and they probably thought this would be a memorable moment for me, which it was, but not in any sort of Hallmark way.

At first it was fun in there, being climbed and licked and nuzzled. It was like being a swizzle stick in a glass of seltzer, with all the puppies bubbling around. But then there was a nip here, a little growl there, and then one puppy peed on my lap.

"Let's take this one," I said and held up the culprit, still dribbling. She looked like a sausage that had been rolled in cotton balls. "It's perfect."

"Make sure it's a girl," my mother said.

"Get a boy dog and the next thing you know he's chasing all the dogs in the neighborhood," my father said. "Next thing you know, the bastards are suing you because your dog knocked up their dog. That's the way it is, you know. People are no good."

"I've got papers," the breeder said. "I'd think people would sue you for *not* letting one of these dogs knock up their dog. These are quality dogs. Show dogs."

My father scowled again, and my mother took out a checkbook and said, "If that one's a girl, we'll take her."

Since there'd been no leg lift involved in the offense, the puppy in question was quickly deemed a girl. I'm not sure how much my mother wrote the check for, but it must have been a lot because all the way home she kept muttering something about the dog costing more than the new linoleum floor she'd been wanting for the kitchen.

We took Tina II home in an old Regent Pop wooden crate my father had lined with a new fuzzy pink blanket. He'd bought a new squeaky pork chop, as well as a squeaky lifelike replica of a severed human foot, complete with a shiny red pedicure. He'd plopped these in the crate, too, along with a windup alarm clock.

"They like the ticking," he said. "It reminds them of their mothers."

I'm not sure how my father knew this, but the idea of taking a puppy and replacing its mother with an alarm clock seemed sad. Still, even though I was very young, I tended to think that dogs were dogs and people were people and that my father's insistence on the Tinas' superiority to all humankind wasn't quite right.

Sure, I'd had my own moments with Tina I—the time I set her ears in sponge rollers; the time I made her wear a birthday hat and try to blow out the candles on the cake my father special-ordered from Guentert's, the best bakery in Braddock; the time I shared her box of Milk-Bones; the time I dressed her up in doll's clothes and made her dance on her hind legs to "Sugar, Sugar," by the Archies. I was, after all, an only child. Sometimes I was lonely and desperate. There were plenty of nights when I'd wept into Tina I's soft black fur and found comfort there.

And things with Tina II weren't much different. When

I'd come home from school, she and my mother would hide and I'd have to find them. Usually, their hiding places were predictable—bedroom closet, living room closet, under the dining room table—but I'd make a big deal of looking. This worked up Tina II into a predictable frenzy, and when she couldn't take it any longer, she'd break out of her hiding place and do sprints around the house. Then she'd jump as high as she could—as high as any performing circus poodle I'd ever seen on TV—and throw her puffball body into mine until I picked her up and let her lick my face.

I loved my dog. I let her sleep with me. I shared lollipops with her and let her eat off my plate. I talked to her like she was a baby, even though I knew she wasn't human at all.

It's that knowing that seemed to be the line between me and my father when it came to our family dog. My father, who did not cook or do groceries, would stop after a ten-hour day in the machine shop to pick up plastic containers full of bloody chicken hearts or gizzards at Foodland. Then he'd fry or boil these and hand-feed them to Tina II while she sat in his chair at the head of the kitchen table.

"You have to prime her," he'd say, as if he'd just give her a taste and then let her go to it on her own.

But the idea of Tina II stuffing her head into a dog dish seemed undignified to my father, and so he'd hand-feed her every meal. He'd give her baths in the bathtub and scrub her down with baby shampoo because the evergreen-smelling dog shampoo my mother bought was too harsh and made Tina II break out in a belly rash.

When Zsa Zsa Gabor made the news for throwing bottles of dog shampoo and attacking a groomer who'd run out of her poodle's favorite brand of five-hundred-dollar Japanese imported flea dip, my father didn't go into his usual rant.

"Five hundred bucks," he said. "That's a lot for shampoo."

Although he himself was interested only in the news, my father would sometimes tune the TV to shows he thought the dog might like. There were shows where the froufrou poodles had cameos, like *The Beverly Hillbillies* and the occasional episode of *The Wonderful World of Disney*. And of course, there was *Lassie*.

By the early 1970s, most people were over *Lassie*, and the show was limping along in syndication in its final seasons. But for my father and our dog, the show was still a must-see.

My father liked TV that confirmed his ideas about the world. This was why he watched the news, since people never failed to disappoint him in the disaster and doom department. And he loved *Lassie* because it showed beyond any doubt that dogs were smarter and classier than people.

"That Jimmy is a chronic complainer," my father would say, though he pronounced *chronic* as *chronie*. Jimmy, of course, was Jimmy Fredericks, the boy with the lame right leg whom Lassie meets in the show's final season.

"Look how Lassie shows him what's what."

Considering that I'd been born with clubbed feet and for years my own legs were often in casts and braces, I didn't appreciate my father calling Jimmy a "whiny gimp." Still, I had to agree that Jimmy was annoying. The whole show was annoying, in that horrible 1950s fluffy righteous kind of way. By the early 1970s, no one other than Jimmy and his *Lassie* cronies said "gee" or "gosh" or ate their peas. And in real life, no one I knew, even in my elementary school, was naive enough to think that a collie would save us all.

In the show's later years, though, that wasn't the point. Lassie, it seems, had moved beyond saving people and was much more interested in saving other animals instead—a fact that my father could respect.

Take the "Peace Is Our Profession" episodes from 1972, for example. Over the course of four episodes, Lassie visits an air force base where she— Okay, actually Lassie was a male collie whose stunt doubles were often female and whose offscreen companions were two female miniature poodles named Buttons and Bows. Anyway, at this air base, Lassie meets a goose who's laid her eggs in a missile launching area. Lassie tries to protect the goose from an imminent missile launch. Lassie saves the goose and her eggs, then befriends a diabetic poodle named Sparky. Sparky stows away on a military plane to be with his owner. There is no insulin on the plane. Sparky is in danger! Lassie, through a series of insistent barks and paw motions, gets permission for the plane to land early and saves Sparky.

"Animals know," my father would say. "They understand things. Don't tell me that dog's not smart."

When the cameras would move in on Lassie for a
melodramatic close-up, my father would find his proof.

"Look at those goddamn eyes. Oh, that dog's smart all
right. It takes brains to act like that. She's got more brains
in her ass than most people have in their heads," he'd say.
Then he'd roll Tina II over and scratch her belly until her
legs convulsed in spasms.

There on the couch in the dark, his dog at his side,
Lassie bounding across a Technicolor open field, my father
seemed almost content, but he never seemed really happy.
Tina II may have sensed this. She may have been as smart
as my father thought she was, because she licked my father
and leapt at him with more vigor than she spent on anyone else.

"The natural state of the sentient adult is a qualified
unhappiness," F. Scott Fitzgerald once wrote in his essay
"The Crack Up." Happiness "is not the natural thing but
the unnatural—unnatural as the Boom; my recent experience parallels the wave of despair that swept the nation
when the Boom was over."

Fitzgerald was writing about his own breakdown. Like
my father, he'd developed a code to live by. Fitzgerald, in
the throes of a depression he'd likened to the Great
Depression, couldn't bear most people, though he made
exceptions for doctors and certain children.

"I do not any longer like the postman, nor the grocer,
nor the editor, nor the cousin's husband, and he in turn

will come to dislike me, so that life will never be very pleasant again," Fitzgerald wrote. "The sign *Cave Canem* is hung permanently just above my door."

Cave Canem.

Beware the dog.

My father loved that Tina II could sound ferocious. If someone rang our doorbell, my father would encourage her growling and snarling.

"Go get 'em, girl. You show 'em. Get 'em now," he'd say.

Strangers were amazed that, when our door opened, the source of the sound wasn't a pit bull. Poodle experts say that when poodles are allowed to grow their fur long, the poodles themselves become confused and think they're much bigger and fiercer than they actually are. Carvings on Roman tombs in AD 30 showed poodles looking both regally Sphinx-like and fearless, more like bears than cartoon vamps.

When Tina II, like her predecessor, was diagnosed with cancer, she was fourteen years old—human, not dog years. My father refused to have her put to sleep. He believed she deserved a natural death and demanded that the vet give her pain medication and that my mother, the registered nurse, use all her skills to help Tina II through her final days.

I was in my last year of college at the time, so I came home every few weeks. With each visit, my father's decision seemed a bit crueler. The tumor affected the dog's intestines and her hind legs. I saw the disease progress—from general malaise, to vomiting, to limping, to where she could only lie down, then could only lie on her side and pick her head up, then one day she could not pick her head up at all. My parents fed her water and vitamins and pain medicine from a dropper and carried her outside until they gave up and just used disposable diapers.

One evening, when my mother was out and my father was left alone with the dog, he panicked. He was certain that Tina II was in a new and particular kind of pain. With my mother gone, he did something he would never have done otherwise. He called a neighbor. This neighbor was also a nurse, and someone he'd rarely spoken to. When I was in high school, this woman's daughter was crowned homecoming queen and vice president of our senior class. The woman and all three of her daughters were gorgeous, and my father had long ago dismissed the entire family as a bunch of stuck-ups. But he was desperate, and so he called.

He told her it was an emergency. He explained what he needed. And, in a gesture that should have forever redeemed humankind in my father's eyes, this woman came.

When my mother arrived home and found out what had happened, she was furious. And so, of course, she called me.

"Do you know what he did?" she yelled into the phone. "I am never going to be able to show my face on this street again. He's a goddamn lunatic."

My dad had asked this woman, who to him was almost a stranger, to give our dog an enema.

An enema, after all, was my mother's prescription of choice whenever anyone in our family complained of stomach pains. Maybe this was what she learned in nursing school, but now, in a world with so many more civilized options, it just seems creepy. Still, back then, my father, who'd probably been my mother's patient more times than I want to think about, was sure that his dog was suffering and that an enema would help.

I'm still trying to picture the whole scene. My father calling and explaining his situation to the woman, maybe even asking her to make a run to the local pharmacy to pick up the necessary supplies; the woman packing her stethoscope, putting on her coat, and telling her husband, "I'll be back in a little while, honey. I have to give the Jakielas' dog an enema."

"It was no skin off her nose," my father said when he pried the phone away from my mother, who was still ranting in the background. "She's a professional. That's what they do. Dog, human, what does it matter? It's all the same."

After Tina II died and my father dug the second backyard grave, another part of him seemed to freeze up. His love for the two Tinas had, as he saw it, made him vulnerable, and so he swore off pets of all kinds.

"Who needs the aggravation?" he'd say. "I want to be free to pick up and go whenever I want. I don't need another rock around my neck."

He wouldn't even allow live plants in the house because they were too much trouble. "They'll just die," he told my mother. "Waste of money." He bought her a plastic rubber tree with a tag that read LIFELIKE when she complained that the house could use a little color.

But without a pet to coddle, my father found he had

too much empty time, so he soon took up birds instead. Every night after dinner, he'd tear leftover bread into tiny chunks. He'd scoop up birdseed from a huge bag he kept in the garage and go out into the yard, where he'd sit on a rickety lawn chair and watch all the birds in the neighborhood dive-bomb their dinner.

Had my father lived in the city, he might have become one of those crazy people who put peanut butter on their sleeves and birdseed in their laps in the hope that pigeons will crawl all over them. I've never understood bird-love, though I know many people fall for it. As for my father, he liked that the birds in our yard seemed to depend on him. When he'd come out of the garage, bag of bread chunks in hand, they'd screech and chatter, they were that happy.

"Listen to that, would you?" he'd say. "Just listen. Isn't that something?"

Maybe loss, as the Buddhists say, teaches us how to live in this world. Maybe it changes us for the better, teaches us how to love with our hands open and know that everything is a process of letting go. This is something I like to think, though judging by my father, I can't say it's true.

Sometimes, when he was out feeding the birds, his neighbor would drive past and she'd honk and my father would wave. She didn't usually stop to talk, but my father would always say of her, "She's one of the good ones."

As for the birds, he figured Hitchcock got it wrong.

"Look at them," my father would say. "They don't hurt anybody. They're better than most people I know."

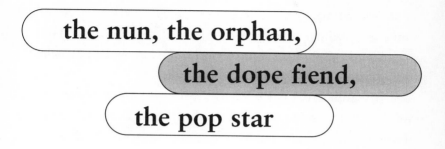

the nun, the orphan, the dope fiend, the pop star

My father's sister was a nun. She was also a regular at Narcotics Anonymous.

"They have their own way of dealing with things like this," my mother said, as if the Catholic Church were the Mafia and my aunt had turned stoolie. "They'll get her straight."

My aunt liked pills. Like everyone else in the family, she liked Iron City Beer. She used to drink it in dainty juice glasses and call it her medicine. I've known this forever, though I'm not sure who told me or why.

My aunt didn't look the pill-popping type. She didn't care much for Vatican II, which said it was okay for nuns to add polyester business suits and Winnie-the-Pooh sweatshirts to their wardrobes.

"It's disgraceful," she said. "A sister should look like a sister. People should know who they're dealing with."

No matter what was going on at my aunt's convent,

when she came to visit, she always wore a full habit—complete with a long black veil and a wimple that blended her chin and her chest in a way that, in profile, made her look like Alfred Hitchcock. On the few occasions that my parents forced me to hug her, she smelled like stale cigarettes and beer, which made me think she drank on duty. This reminded me of bad jokes. *A rabbi, the Easter Bunny, and this nun walk into a bar . . .*

My aunt's real name was Julie, but it probably doesn't matter much since I only heard my father use it a few times. Her chosen name was Sister Joseph, and even though she was my aunt, I called her Sister.

Sister Joseph was a Sister of Mercy, an order that has a special love for the virtue of mercy. In the words of Catherine McAuley, who founded the order in Dublin, Ireland, back in 1831, "Mercy is more than charity for it not only gives benefits, but it receives and pardons again and again—even the ungrateful."

From what I could figure out from late-night phone calls and half-coded discussions during family gatherings, my aunt had gotten her share of mercy-laden indulgences from the church. I'm not sure how the mother superior at her convent first discovered my aunt's addiction, but, then again, if everyone in our family, including me, knew about my aunt's problems, they probably weren't much of a secret.

She had been sent several times to Narcotics Anonymous, then a church treatment center, and was given time off to get well. This went on for years, but not long enough to get a pink slip from the religious life. I always assumed the only way a nun could get the boot would be if she slept with a priest or posed for *Playboy*. Liking painkillers didn't seem like a fireable offense, but then again, things were a little different in my house.

My parents stockpiled pills the way militias stockpile guns. As a nurse, my mother knew the value of good drugs. In a cabinet over our kitchen sink, there were shoe boxes filled with prescription painkillers, sleeping pills, antibiotics, and enough bottles of codeine-laced cough syrup to knock a linebacker on his butt.

Neither my parents nor I were particularly healthy, and so, with my allergies, my father's emphysema, and what my mother referred to as her "nervous problems," we were guaranteed a decent haul anytime one of us went to see a doctor, which was often.

My mother was on hand for all doctors' visits. Whenever doctors would ask about symptoms, my mother, the medical professional, would jump in and rattle off a textbook-perfect list that would make them dole out the good stuff.

"They're stingy, these doctors," she'd say. "You've got to tell them. You've got to talk to them. Otherwise, they'll give you an aspirin and a pat on the head and what good's that?"

My father, who called the Vietnam protestors he saw on TV dope fiends and said things like "the trouble with this younger generation is they're a bunch of hopheads and dope fiends; free love my ass," supported my mother's efforts. He was sure that health care was a racket and all doctors were crooks. When he went to see a doctor, my father wasn't happy unless he walked out with a stack of prescriptions and a bag full of pill samples.

By the time I turned into a teenager, I knew the truth about my middle-aged suburban parents. Sure, they kept their lawn nice and went to church. They paid their bills and sent greeting cards. My mother made cookies and baked bread. My father, no matter how much he hated his job, almost never missed a day of work. And they loved drugs. Not in the way addicts loved drugs, but in the way most people love the things that make them feel most secure. Having boxes full of drugs meant that my parents were ready for whatever crisis might come up.

Around my thirteenth birthday, my dad got one of those late-night phone calls from Sister Joseph. In our house, I could lie in my bed across the hall and listen to everything, including his end of the phone call.

"Oh," he said. "I see," he said. "Well, we got food."

We were doomed.

We got food is code for "come and stay as long as you want" when you're talking to children of the Great Depression, people like my parents and Sister Joseph. These were people who got nostalgic about how scarce food was when they were growing up. They tended to one-up each other over who'd had it worse—whose ribs stuck out far enough to pick your teeth on or whose stomach swelled up like a rotten tomato or whose vitamin deficiency left him looking and smelling like piss right to the eyeballs. And they did this with a kind of reverence that would make people think Norman Rockwell should have painted kids in burlap sacks eating government cheese.

The last time his sister visited, she and my father spent the evening getting sentimental about bug-riddled flour and lard.

"There were bugs in those bags of government flour," she said. "Some of them were fat as grapes."

"I ate bugs," my father said. "I didn't care what they got cooked up in. I ate them."

"You certainly did," she said.

"I ate bugs like they were chocolate chips and I liked it," my father said. "Goddamn bugs."

"And lard," she said. "Don't forget lard."

"Goddamn lard," he said.

"Mother rubbed it on our chests when we were sick, remember?" she said.

"Chests, hell," my father said. "We rubbed it on our bread, Dad rubbed it on his belt, and after he beat the crap out of us, we rubbed it on our sore asses."

It was refreshing the way my father swore and flung God's name around in vain in front of a full-blown bride of Christ, but still, it wasn't enough to make a visit from Sister Joseph worthwhile.

This was what I had to look forward to, I knew, lying in bed, listening to my father go on about the contents of our fridge to his sister, who apparently had fallen so far off the wagon this time that neither she nor the church, all mercies aside, was sure she'd ever get back on.

"It'll be one week, two tops," my father said the next morning as I paced a path through the hot pink shag rug in my bedroom, which I was going to have to give over to Sister Joseph because, according to my mother, Sister Joseph needed her privacy. Sister Joseph had a bad back and couldn't sleep on the couch. According to my mother, Sister Joseph was having a hard time. Sister Joseph would need her sleep.

From every corner of the room, Shaun Cassidy, in his many *Tiger Beat* and *Teen Beat* centerfolds, stared down at my father and me. Shaun, looking French in his red-and-white-striped sailor shirt and jaunty beret. Shaun, looking sexy onstage in a puffy blue blouse and extra-feathery hair. Vulnerable Shaun in a satin bomber jacket cuddling a teddy bear. Seaworthy Shaun, in a captain's hat, shirt unbuttoned to show off a buttery, hairless chest on a fishing boat somewhere off the coast of Florida. Rock 'n' roll porn Shaun, completely shirtless, his nipples exposed like two gumdrops.

Just a few months before, my father had taken me and Chris Grande to see Shaun Cassidy live at the Civic Arena in Pittsburgh. During the forty-five-minute drive from Trafford to downtown Pittsburgh, my poor father had to listen to Chris and me battle over who loved Shaun more, who knew more Shaun trivia, and who, having held her breath without cheating all the way through the Squirrel Hill Tunnel, was going to bear Shaun's children. Before we came to blows over which pinkie Shaun wore his traditional family crest ring on (his right), my father pulled into the arena's parking lot, where he promptly gave us each a few dollars to spend on concert paraphernalia.

Chris bought an autographed postcard and an official Shaun Cassidy stickpin. I gave a Moonie two dollars for a rose.

Considering I never made it to an airport until I was seventeen, this was the first real Moonie I'd ever seen. Still, he seemed suspiciously muscular for someone who supposedly lived on sprouts and tofu. With his shiny bald head and ropy forearms, he looked a little like Mr. Clean, if Mr. Clean wore a bedsheet and sandals and had long toenails.

"I'm going to give this to Shaun Cassidy," I told my Moonie friend as I dug around in his bucket of wilting roses looking for one that had at least most of its petals intact. "I love Shaun Cassidy."

"Maybe you should buy two," he said, handing me a pamphlet that I supposed offered a step-by-step guide to turning Moonie. "Just to let him know how much you love him."

I figured one rose would do and besides, I was saving what little cash I had left for one of those glamorous glow-in-the-dark choker/headbands. Still, as the proud owner of a fully functioning Ouija board, I was open-minded where religion was concerned. I took the Moonie's pamphlet, even though I was afraid to look at it, just in case my father was watching.

Inside the arena, we had great floor seats, three rows from the stage. We had plenty of space to scream and dance and tear our hair. When Shaun came back with an encore of "Da Doo Ron Ron," I hurled my limp-stemmed rose in the air. It fell on the floor one row in front of me and was promptly stomped to death.

"Don't worry, princess," my father said in the car on the drive back home. Chris had passed out in the backseat, where she made sucking noises and cuddled her SHAUN CASSIDY LIVE T-shirt against her face.

"I saw him. I really did. He was looking at you and smiling. Now that was something, princess, really something."

This is how it was with my father and me back then. Whatever his faults and no matter how gruff he was on a usual day. I loved my father and felt, in moments like this one, that he was the only person in the world who would ever understand me.

"I can't believe you're doing this," I said, and he started to backtrack on his estimate of Sister Joseph's stay.

"A week or so, that's it," my father said. "Hey, she's family."

This was, of course, part of the problem. Sister Joseph, like the rest of my parents' family members, was old school. She believed that blood was blood. This presented some problems for me, considering I was adopted.

Whenever she came for a visit, Sister Joseph would constantly draw attention to this fact.

"You should get down on your knees and thank God you have such wonderful parents who would take you out of that orphanage," she'd say.

"You would have grown up eating garbage," she'd say at dinner, "if your parents didn't take you out of that orphanage."

"Think of how it would be in that orphanage," she'd

say if she'd hear me complain about my wardrobe. "You should get down on your knees and thank God you're not wearing rags."

In short, whenever Sister Joseph visited, she treated me like a charity case. And even if I was a charity case, I didn't like to hear about it.

Where adoption was concerned, my parents and I didn't dwell much. The story goes like this:

My parents were in their thirties when they adopted me—older than most of my classmates' parents and older than most adoption agencies would have liked back in 1964. Still, my mother had already had one near-fatal miscarriage. Both she and my father wanted a baby and they wouldn't be discouraged.

"We wouldn't take no for an answer," my father would say. "The bastards would have liked us to just turn around and walk out, but we weren't going nowhere."

Luckily, I was a bargain-basement case. Born with badly clubbed feet, I needed both quick placement and special care. Had my parents insisted on a healthy white baby girl, they would have been put on a long waiting list, and, given their age, they probably wouldn't have gotten a baby at all. But considering my special circumstances, plus the fact that my mother was a nurse and was seen as specially equipped to deal with a case like mine, we were matched up within months.

Shortly after my first birthday, my parents plucked me out of Rosalia Foundling Home, the Catholic orphanage and home for unwed mothers in Pittsburgh. Several years and many surgeries later, I was running laps in the back-yard and driving my parents, biological or not, insane.

Like I said, we didn't dwell on any of it much. Okay, I was blond and green-eyed in a family that, on one side, was swarthy and Italian looking and prone to getting the map of Italy tattooed on their forearms, and, on the other, bowl-faced and pasty and fluently Polish. So I liked books and music and had an inexplicable love for big cities, New York in particular, in a blue-collar, small-town family.

I always knew two things growing up: My parents, whatever their faults, loved me. And I was adopted. Believing it was better if I knew everything from the very beginning, my parents told me all they knew about my circumstances, including my birth name—Amelia Phelan. We were comfortable enough to make jokes about things that I knew, from reading *Reader's Digest* and talking to other adoptees at school, were considered sensitive.

"I don't know where you came from," my mother said once when she discovered that, while she'd been at work, I'd rearranged her kitchen cabinets and sorted her spices by color.

"Me neither," I said.

"Phelan means wolf," I told my mother one day, having looked it up at school.

"Well, you're not being raised by them," she said, "so clean up your room."

When the subject of adoption came up, my mother would usually be the one to do it, mostly because of those *Reader's Digest* articles, which said she should help me feel comfortable with my real identity.

When it came time for my Catholic confirmation and I had the chance to choose a new name, my mother had an idea.

"Why don't you use Joan?" she said. Joan, I knew, was my birth mother's name. "It will make you feel connected to your past. It's a good saint's name, too. You can't go wrong with Joan."

"No way," I said. What I didn't tell her was that my friend Muttsy was already going with Joan, and besides, I had something more unique in mind.

"Deanna," I told Sister Lucilla when she asked. Sister Lucilla, aka Sister Lucifer, was the principal at St. Regis Elementary. She was also in charge of the details for confirmation.

"Who's this Deanna?" she asked, looking me over, from my shoes to my eyebrows. Sister Lucilla had this way of checking everyone out, as if a lie were visible, like an ink stain or dandruff.

"She was burned at the stake," I said. "Don't tell me you don't know about her? She's very famous."

There was no St. Deanna, and therefore the name was technically off limits as far as my confirmation went. But Shaun Cassidy had this song, "Hey Deanie," and, well, you know.

"You don't say?" Lucilla said.

"Yes, it was awful," I said. "Just like Joan of Arc, except Deanna was from Ireland, of course. Everyone knows."

I don't know why, but for once, Lucilla bought what I

was selling and wrote down my new name: Lori Lynn
Deanna Jakiela.

"You sound like a state," my friend Gigi said. "Lori
Lynn Deanna. St. Indiana. That's good."

Gigi had blond pigtails. She liked to please everyone,
Lucilla included. Her confirmation name was Mary.

"You know, as in the mother of God," she said.

"Kiss ass," I said.

I dreaded Sister Joseph's visits because she made me feel
guilty. Not just for something I did, like stealing a jar of
paste back in first grade, but for my life.

Guilt was a given if you grew up Catholic, there was
no way around that. But having a nun in the family really
upped the ante. Having a nun in the family who considered you an outsider and thereby open to even greater
scrutiny made things worse. Still, there were ways to push
the envelope.

Take me cursing at Gigi, for instance. Even in the
Catholic Church, I found that there are ways to get your
point across while still appearing to color inside the lines.

"Kiss ass," I told Gigi, is totally legitimate, since *ass*
appears in both the dictionary and the Bible.

Hell was fine, too. Also in the Bible. When I felt the
most desperate need to swear—say, in math class—I'd
learned a trick with a calculator. Punch in 7734 and hold
the calculator upside down and it does your swearing for
you.

Bitch was fine, too—in the dictionary, female dog. And

cock, as in rooster, and *pussy*, as in kitty, were technically okay, although they made me uncomfortable.

Pussy, in particular, was a problem.

All her life, my mother has been oblivious to sexual double entendre. And so, when I was in kindergarten and she got the great idea to dress us both up as matching leopards, in footed leopard-print pajamas with stuffed pantyhose legs for tails, she never counted on the fallout. She started calling us both pussies. She was Big Pussy. I was Little Pussy. She sometimes shortened this to Puss. Sure, the leopard costumes were cute and maybe even the hit of the neighborhood that year, but the nicknames stuck and by the time I approached puberty, they took on a whole new dimension.

Like a lot of mothers, my mother put notes in my lunchbox. Unlike other mothers, my mother's notes had a cat theme. They were addressed to Little Pussy. They were signed, Love, Big Pussy. Sometimes they said, "Have a great day!" and sometimes they were written in cat-speak: "Have a meow-meow good day" or "You're purrrrfect."

This was all very sweet and cute until one day when Mark Capolli, who'd been horribly teased for years because he was fat and smelled, got hold of one of these notes and, in the manner of people who've been bullied all their lives, was happy to turn the attention to me.

"Here pussy pussy, here little puss," he and his skinny pimple-faced crony Bill Orwich would shout in the lunchroom. "Puss Puss Puss," they'd write on notes they'd pass around class.

"Go to hell," I'd say, and pray Sister Lucilla wasn't around to hear.

With Sister Joseph around, there would be no swearing. No loose boy talk around the house. No loud rock music. No revealing clothes. The latter included my favorite tight, scoop-neck, hot pink T-shirt with the iron-on decal of a stop sign and the words: STOP. I LOVE IT.

Having a nun living in my bedroom was definitely going to cramp my style. Still, in the days leading up to her visit, it was interesting to watch my parents squirm as well.

My mother dusted, sprayed everything with lemon polish, then redusted. She scrubbed things with bleach. Once, when I got up to get a glass of water in the middle of the night, she was in the kitchen on her hands and knees, scrubbing between the floor tiles with a toothbrush.

"We just want to make it nice for her," my mother said, though I knew she was worried about Sister Joseph judging her as well.

If we had stopped to think, my mother and I would have figured out that Sister Joseph might have been just as worried about us judging her, considering the circumstances surrounding her visit.

"It's not that I don't trust her," my mother said as she shoved a case of beer and a box filled with liquor bottles under the basement stairs. "It's just better if there's no temptation."

That my mother thought of such things as temptations and not evidence says a lot about her own peculiar way of seeing. If Sister Joseph had prayed not to be led into temptation, coming to our house was a cruel trick. My parents were, after all, their own pharmacy. Bringing Sister Joseph into our house in her fragile state was like inviting Al Capone into a bank after hours.

"It's not that I don't trust her," my mother said, when I caught her piling the shoe boxes full of prescription pill bottles behind a mound of stuffed animals in my closet. "It's just that I think it's safer this way."

My mother, a smart woman, sometimes lacked criminal sense. Since she was the one who was forcing me to give Sister Joseph my bedroom, you'd think she'd have hidden the drugs in another part of the house. Maybe she figured the stuffed animals would throw her off. Who would expect to find Valium tucked under a pile of Snoopys and teddy bears?

I think my mother fell asleep during those made-for-TV movies where, for a while, anything that was smuggleable—drugs, explosives, top-secret microfilm—was stuffed into a smug-looking teddy bear. "No one will ever look here," the criminal mastermind would say, cackling in an evil criminal mastermind way as he stitched up Teddy's butt.

When Sister Joseph arrived at our house, in her usual full-blown habit, dragging a big black suitcase, I was surprised to find I'd used up all my dread. And when my mother gave me a covert shove, I leaned in and hugged her, my face getting lost once again in the black folds of her dress. She smelled, as usual, like cigarettes and beer. But she seemed quieter, more reserved, and for whatever reason, she held back on telling me I should be thankful for my life. I don't know why. Maybe she was feeling vulnerable herself. Maybe she was tired. Maybe she was just getting older and forgetting things.

And even though it was inherently creepy having a nun in the house, I didn't think too much about it until that first night, at bedtime, when I retired to the couch in my mother's sewing room and Sister Joseph locked herself in my bedroom. I could picture her in there, still in her full nun getup, all nice and comfy under my pink canopy, surrounded by Shaun Cassidy and my favorite black-velvet poster that advised, IF YOU LOVE SOMETHING, SET IT FREE.

Who knows what she thought about in there, before she went to sleep, surrounded by everything I loved and had, at least for the moment, set free.

I hoped she wasn't touching things, that she wasn't rooting around to find my diary or the pulp paperback I'd been keeping under my bed. I'd found the paperback on the G. C. Murphy's bargain table, where you could buy five paperbacks for a dollar. The books' covers were torn off, and I tended to snatch them up at random without reading more than the title or a few sentences. I'd lucked out on this one, which turned out to be about a character named Del Sade and a virgin named Claire who discovered that she liked it when Del Sade spanked her snowy bum and tied her up, or forced her to strip naked and run a gauntlet full of his lusty young manservants. My parents, especially my mother, would kill me if they ever found the book, but I couldn't bear to get rid of it.

I couldn't imagine what Sister Joseph would do if she came across the book. I couldn't imagine her ever being curious about sex, or ever having been young or a girl or anything like me. I don't know what she might have loved back when she was just Julie, back before she discovered God. I don't know what her favorite color might have been before everything went black, before her parents had pushed her into the convent because, as my father put it, "it made the family look good to have someone on the inside."

They must have had something in common, Sister Joseph and my father, because whenever she needed him, he was there to help her. And even though he called her The Penguin behind her back, my father was tender with his sister.

"She's having a hard time," he told me. "So be nice for once. Okay?"

And I was, or at least I tried. Since I couldn't resist one grand gesture of rebellion, I made it a subtle one. Before Sister Joseph arrived, I'd moved my stereo into the basement. During her stay, I played Billy Joel's "Only the Good Die Young" over and over, belting out the parts about Catholic girls starting much too late until my mother made me stop.

Several times during her stay, I had to go into my room to get clean clothes. One day, Sister Joseph's black suitcase was open on the floor and inside, along with her rosary beads and what looked like a spare habit, there was a pair of panties and a bra. The panties were white high-risers, like my mother's, but the bra had a bit of lace on the straps and one pink rosebud at the center. The bra was dainty and girl-like and unexpectedly shocking.

For years, I'd watched Sister Joseph do the things humans do—eat, drink, fall asleep midsentence. But she was a nun, and therefore separate from the rest of us. Nuns did not have lacy underwear. Then again, nuns weren't supposed to pop painkillers and get fall-down drunk, either, so there you go.

At first, I felt bad about snooping in her suitcase. But after she left and I moved back into my bedroom, I found that Sister Joseph had indeed been doing some snooping of her own. My diary was still in its place, hidden behind my dresser, and my novel was still under my bed, hidden by a mound of shoes. But when my mother dug her pill shoe boxes out of the closet, a few bottles were missing.

"Christ," she said.

This, of course, was in character. Sister Joseph was, after all, "having a hard time." That's what my father said. But what was out of character was that bra, with its little candy-button rose, which she wore hidden under layer after layer of regulation black.

Since seeing the contents of Sister Joseph's suitcase had convinced me that she was, after all, an underwear-toting member of the human race, I started to think that whatever she saw in my room might have made her see me differently, too. I took an inventory—my Beach Boys records, the *Tiger Beat* posters, my cola-flavored lip gloss, my favorite crushed-blue-velvet-button-fly-hip-hugger-bell-bottom jeans. I wondered what these things, taken in all at once, said about me. Not much, I guess, but back then I hoped that, in some way, they would have made Sister Joseph see me as something other than an orphan child who needed to be grateful.

I thought it was a good sign that, when Sister Joseph left after two weeks, she sent my parents and me small gifts. My father got a medallion with an embossed image of St. Jude, the patron saint of lost causes and an excellent choice when it came to confirmation names. My mother got a lace handkerchief and a set of handmade doilies. I got a gold cross necklace and a note that read, "You're a good girl. Thank you. God bless."

Then again, people don't really change much.

Sister Joseph would die two years later—cancer, I think, not an overdose—just a few months after she'd sent me a Christmas card that read, "Be thankful to God for your life. You wouldn't be able to walk if your parents didn't take you out of that home."

Well then.

Back in 1978, Shaun Cassidy told *Rolling Stone*: "I hate bubblegum music. I think it's pablum and I will not make a record like that." He thought he was more like the Ramones, intensity-wise, and was stunned that he hadn't gotten a Grammy.

"No one takes you seriously if you're on television," he said, talking about *The Hardy Boys*, a show that consistently beat out *The Wonderful World of Disney* when it came to numbers of viewers. "You become one dimensional. A joke."

On *The Hardy Boys*, Shaun played Joe Hardy, the headstrong, free-spirited, but all-around good guy. Parker Stevenson, who was twenty-seven years old at the time, played his brother Frank. Frank was cooler, more levelheaded. Neither Hardy ever slipped out of character. They were completely predictable, and every week, when audiences tuned in, they knew what to expect.

Rolling Stone described *Hardy Boys* episodes this way: "Hardys meet girl. Girl meets crisis. Hardys solve crisis. Hardys make friends with girl."

Sometimes I wish life were like that. Steady. Earnest. Simple as a pop song.

But if there's anything I learned from Sister Joseph, it's that life and the people in it are mostly complicated. We might all be jokes, but there are a lot of punch lines and we don't always see them coming.

The pope, a piece of string, a blonde, an Irish man, a black man, a nun, a rabbi, the Easter bunny, the tooth fairy, and a midget walk into a bar. The bartender says, "Hold on, this has to be a joke."

We don't fit into neat categories, we don't see ourselves clearly, and, even if we dress the part, there's a good chance we've been miscast.

This goes for me and everyone I've ever met, with the exception of Sister Lucilla, who was, as far as I can tell, the church-approved incarnation of pure evil.

When I was in sixth grade, Sister Lucilla did double

duty as both the principal and our music/phys. ed. teacher. One day, when we were supposed to be practicing harmonies on "This Little Light of Mine," some of the boys snuck under the concert risers. They were probably just goofing off, but Sister Lucilla believed the worst. She was sure they were trying to look up the girls' skirts, including her own. She dragged the needle across the record we'd been singing along with, then stood silent for a moment, glaring at us all. She focused her rage first on one boy, then another, as they crept out from under the risers. Finally, she settled on Ken O'Connor, whose face had turned as red as his hair.

"Oh, now you're embarrassed," she said. "How perfect."

What Sister Lucilla did next did more for the cause of celibacy than any sex-education class ever could. She lifted up her regulation black nun skirt and showed our entire class her girdle.

It was a terrifying thing—industrial, a heavy panel job, all yellowed and worn. Her black stockings were anchored to the girdle with thick garters that dangled like tongues. Both the girdle and the elasticized stockings were so tight her thighs, which were all cottage cheese and shot through with lumpy, mold-colored veins, poufed out.

"So there," she said, mercifully letting her skirt drop back down. "Now you see what's what."

when a junior miss
walks down the street

When I was two, I won second place in a beautiful-baby contest at Sears. The prize was a museum-size framed photo of me, plus a set of steak knives.

"The contest was fixed," my father told friends and neighbors. "Second place? Who are they kidding with that? But these knives. You can cut tin cans with these sons of bitches."

For years, my mother insisted on keeping the gigantic baby picture prominently displayed in the dining room. She liked to tell dinner guests the story of my near miss, how she pinned my lacy designer dress to the casts on my clubbed feet and spit-curled my thin strands of hair into what looked like a baby comb-over.

"I thought about getting her a wig," she'd say, half joking. "But they didn't make one small enough."

It took years for me to grow into whatever image my mother thought was suitable and trophy-worthy. Finally, by the time I turned seventeen and told my mother I wanted to enter the Pennsylvania Junior Miss pageant, she figured my chances at winning this time around were pretty good.

"You have more hair now," she said.

This is how I ended up parading around Fairgrounds Square Mall in Reading, Pennsylvania, being led by a crazed-clownish woman named Darla, the official pageant publicist. Darla wore a Pepto-Bismol-colored suit and matching pumps, and her hair was done up in a lacquered bouffant. She had a nervous twitch that made her cock her head first to one side, then the other, which is probably why she reminded me of one of those spring-necked poodles people stick on their dashboards, the kind of thing my father said caused accidents.

"Come on, chop chop, and sit on Santa's lap," Darla said, clapping her hands. "Chop chop. And don't forget, girls. You're Junior Misses! Now, smi-yull."

This particular photo op brought photographers from both the *Reading Eagle* and the *Reading Times*. Even WTVE and the other local television stations had shown up.

There were thirty of us, all high school seniors, all dudded up in our business-casual best. For me, this meant a red-velvet blazer, a pleated polyester skirt, and a pink blouse with huge magenta-tipped ruffles. We were vying for the title of 1982 Pennsylvania Junior Miss.

The photo op, which involved each of us sitting on the lap of a lascivious-looking Santa whose red cap and curls were pulled down low on his forehead, gangster-style, was just the first of a weeklong series of humiliations that would include marching through malls like this one singing the Junior Miss cheer, with Darla leading us like a drum major:

> *Oh when a Junior Miss walks down the street,*
> *She looks a hundred per from head to feet.*
> *She's got that style, that smile, that winning way.*
> *And when you look at her, you'll recognize her and*
>   *you'll say,*
> *Now there's a girl I'd like to know*
> *She's got that Junior Miss sparkle, pep and glow*
> *And just to look at her is quite a treat,*
> *It can't be beat, a Junior Miss*
> *Hey!*

I tried hard not to get caught lip-synching, since I couldn't bear to belt that cheer out in public. Still, even when Darla's incessant hand-clapping and the media's interest seemed odd, I have to admit I was dazzled by pageant life. My fellow contestants were, too. From the moment we arrived at the Abraham Lincoln Motor Inn in downtown Reading and got our first taste of the local paparazzi, we all bought the idea that, for a week at least, we were famous.

I ended up as part of the Junior Miss crowd mostly by default. My boyfriend's mother, Donna, had told me about the pageant—she'd been a judge or something like that years before. Donna pumped her own gas, had twice divorced her no-good husband, wore flashy business suits with shoulder pads the size of toasters, and worked in a high-rise office building in downtown Pittsburgh.

In her spare time, Donna was an expert at Trivial Pursuit and spent a lot of time on her couch drinking wine and eating pints of ice cream with chocolate sprinkles. Once, when my über-strict parents briefly kicked me out of their house for kissing Donna's son on the living room couch, Donna let me move into her basement. She even called my mother, who was menopausal and predictably hysterical, to ask, "Were their clothes on or off?" When my mother told her "on," Donna said simply, "Well, then, what's there to worry about?"

My mother thought Donna was disgusting. I thought she was wonderful. Whenever Donna gave me advice, I tended to take it.

"You're perfect," she said. "The judges will love you. The money's yours already."

Junior Miss pageants are scholarship pageants. Thousands of college dollars are at stake, and great emphasis is placed on the talent competition and a question-and-answer session with the judges.

When interviewed by *Reading Times* reporter George Berkin, Miss Butler County Kristy White, who looked like a cross between Snow White and Joanie from *Happy Days*, revealed the answer that had won her the title.

"They asked about my first kiss. They wanted details," she said, giggling. "I just said it was nice."

My judges were slightly less voyeuristic. Instead of asking about my love life, they made me identify world lead-ers from news photos and talk about what they meant to me. I think I won because I recognized Mikhail Gorbachev, which wasn't hard, given his birthmark and all. I said I thought he could do a lot for world peace.

At Junior Miss, there is no swimsuit competition. There is, however, a more refined substitute, "Poise and Appearance," or P and A. P and A requires contestants to twirl around in evening wear and model outfits they made themselves.

Back in the 1980s, feminism had yet to infiltrate Junior Miss pageants. Simplicity Patterns and Kraft Foods were both big sponsors, and contestants were expected to know their way around both a stove and a sewing machine. I had already nearly failed home ec class twice—once for setting a tin of madeleines on fire, and once for hopelessly jamming my high school's prized new Singer Elite while trying to hem an apron. This was not promising.

For the cooking competition, I whipped up spinach dip. My three-ingredient gem (a secret blend of powdered onion soup mix, sour cream, and frozen spinach) had always seemed festive nestled in its hollowed-out pumpernickel loaf. My aunts, who believed that, due to my domestic dyslexia, I'd never amount to anything, lavished praise on me whenever I'd bring the dip to family gatherings.

"How ever did you do this?" they'd say. "Did you scoop out the bread with your own hands? Oh, do tell us more."

But compared with the other contestants' entries— Miss Bucks County's homemade apple cobbler or Miss

Dauphin County's petite pastries in raspberry chocolate sauce, for example—my signature dip was a lumpy, alga-laden bog.

As for my Simplicity outfits, I somehow put together, without staples or superglue, two shapeless jumpers, one pink and one gray, with big square patch pockets that made my hips look huge. One other Junior Miss—Miss Greater Abington, I think—who listed sewing among her interests, made her own Scarlett O'Hara evening gown, complete with a satin bustle and a parasol.

"What I love about Simplicity patterns," she'd told the judges, winking coyly behind the lacy edges of her parasol, "is that they're simple."

But I'm getting ahead here.

Despite my obvious lack of Junior Miss DNA, I wanted to go to school for journalism and had been eyeballing Syracuse University. But it was out of state and, my parents said, out of the question. I'd told Donna about my dreams, and the next thing I knew, I was signing Junior Miss waivers that said I wouldn't hold the pageant responsible if I injured myself or others along the way.

Unfortunately, I lived in Trafford, a town the size and significance of belly lint tucked in Westmoreland County. Westmoreland County doesn't have a Junior Miss, per se, and so I was considered an At-Large contestant. Being At-Large sounded both criminal and seedy, like I was on the lam or had crashed a party full of contestants from more legitimate counties like Berks and Schuylkill.

The local competition for Miss At-Large was held in

an office building somewhere in New Kensington. The whole thing—even when the judges pronounced me the winner—felt like a doctor's visit. There was no sash, no tiara, no big local scholarship bucks. Just some hand-shakes and a slip of paper that said I was on my way to the state finals.

Another problem with being At-Large is that you have to find sponsors to cover the cost of everything from your plane ticket to your evening gown. Throughout my years in Girl Scouts, dance teams, and marching bands, my parents had always been the type to buy twenty hoagies or three dozen candy bars during fund-raisers so I wouldn't have to peddle door-to-door.

"What do they think you are, a beggar?" my father would growl as he'd hand over fifty or sixty dollars for waxy chocolate or slabs of greasy lunch meat. "No kid of mine is going around looking for handouts."

For the week after a fund-raiser, my father would eat soggy hoagies for lunch and dinner. He'd store candy bars in the freezer until they turned chalk gray.

Even though entering the Junior Miss pageant had been Donna's idea, my parents, and particularly my moth-er, who felt Sears cheated her all those years ago, had sup-ported the plan.

And so, when I won the local competition, my parents had already decided they'd foot the bill. Since I had to list something official on the forms, my father told me to write down Radform Tool, the machine shop where he worked, as the sponsor.

My father, of course, would never allow me to actually call Radform Tool's owners and ask them for real sponsorship.

"They're cockroaches," he said. "We don't need their filthy money. They can eat shit and die."

For years, he told stories of shop supervisors with stopwatches who would follow workers like my dad into the bathroom, then deduct the minutes and seconds spent "on break" from the workers' time cards. He'd talk about men who'd lose fingers or an eye or worse, then have to foot their own medical bills because the shop supervisors—backed by company insurance investigators—claimed the men had been careless.

Growing up, I always thought my father exaggerated how bad things were at Radform, the way I assumed he exaggerated how bad his life was during the Depression. I bought his stories about eating lard and bugs, since his sister, the nun, had backed him up. But I didn't believe, for example, that my father ever wore burlap underwear or a pair of shoes made from cereal boxes. I didn't believe that he and his eight siblings slept sardine-style in one bed, or that, until he met my mother, he thought ketchup was spaghetti sauce.

As for his Radform stories, I knew he hated his job and that he had never planned this life for himself. I figured he just pushed things a bit to show everyone else how miserable he really was.

But once, in August the summer before the pageant, my father forgot his lunch at home and my mother asked me to take it to him.

My father was working in graphite that day, which meant he was in the back of the shop. I had to go around the building and pound on a huge garage door, hoping he could hear me over the noise of the machines. Somehow, he did, and when the garage door rolled open, a gust of heat and ash came out, along with my father, his eyes and teeth gleaming in contrast to the soot on his skin.

"Hi there, princess," he said. "Thanks for the eats."

I'm not sure if this is really what I saw, or if my memory has added some things to make the place match what I felt that day. But whenever I think of my father on that loading dock, taking the brown paper bag with its two bologna sandwiches, one mottled banana, and a heart-shaped note from my mother inside, I see fire. It's behind my father, deep inside the shop, and it's the only light. There's a thick smell of burning metal and sweat and I think this is what hell would look and smell like if there were such a place.

When I drove away, in my rearview mirror I could see my father turn to go back inside. The garage door rolled down behind him, and for a moment I thought I'd never see him again.

Although he'd always had plans to get out, my father would stay at Radform for more than twenty years. He'd retire with a flimsy benefits package, a tie clip, and a fake gold watch that he'd never wear because it would make his wrist break out in a rash.

You might think, having already had a window into my father's life, that I would have understood him better back when I was seventeen. But I didn't. Instead of realizing what it meant for my father to buy me a plane ticket to Reading—my first time on an airplane—not to mention those various business-casual getups and an evening gown, I felt like a fraud.

I didn't want Radform Tool Company, legitimate or not, to be listed as my sponsor. The other girls, many of whom were pageant veterans, were sponsored by their local Jaycees, Lions Clubs, and chambers of commerce. One was even sponsored by Coca-Cola, which made her seem unbeatable. And even though there were a few other odd sponsors—Radform could hold its own with, say, Orange Julius or Eat 'n Park—I felt from the very beginning that I was going somewhere I didn't belong.

And so it shouldn't have been a surprise that I got lost at Pittsburgh International Airport and nearly missed my flight. Or that, during the flight, I couldn't stop sneezing and my ears felt like someone had jammed pencils into them. Or that, later that first night, during a media dinner and orientation at St. Matthew's United Methodist Church, I'd be seated next to a pageant judge when I'd discover that I'd left a huge pink sponge roller in my hair. Or that, during a lunch at The Optimist Club, I would be seated next to this same judge when my new friend Joann, Bucks County's Junior Miss, would start pointing to her eyebrow. It took a while for me to get the hint and reach up to find a huge piece of baked potato stuck in mine.

Let's just say, during the entire week, I was never a

hundred per, no matter how loud Darla cheered. While dressed up as one of Snow White's dwarfs for a dance routine to "Whistle While You Work," I nearly took another Junior Miss's eye out with my plastic pickax.

Mostly, I found my troubles very funny. I giggled a lot, which didn't endear me to the newspaper reporters who asked questions like "How has your life changed since you became a Junior Miss?" and "What's the most important life lesson you've learned through this experience?"

But as the pageant competition crept closer, I began to feel a sense of doom. I started to wonder if my father had been right years ago, if these things were all fixed, if the odds were hopelessly against people like me. Still, I kept at it, and visions of scholarship dollars, proud parents, fame, fortune, and, most important, escape to someplace wonderful like Syracuse kept me going.

There was, of course, the talent competition, the one area I felt I could do well in. I'd been playing the piano since I was in third grade and was going to do an excerpt from Mendelssohn's Scherzo, a difficult, raging piece that I'd practiced and memorized and dreamed of playing while I slept. Three of the other girls were doing vocal solos of "Out Here on My Own" from *Fame*. Another one was twirling batons and swords to "ABC, 1-2-3" by the Jackson Five. There were the usual jazz/tap specialists, and even one mime.

Classical piano, I figured, trumped mimes, at least.

The night before the pageant, our parents were allowed to join us in Reading. Up until then, we'd been sequestered like a jury from our family and friends. But this particular Thursday was, after all, Thanksgiving, and Darla saw publicity opportunities in the homecoming.

My parents drove up in the Chrysler. My mother said my father had stayed up the night before, coating it with Turtle Wax and tinkering with the near-perfect engine.

"It's in mint condition," my father reported. "Purrs like a goddamn kitten."

All the contestants and families got together for a Turkey Dinner Smorgasbord at the Abraham Lincoln Motor Inn. Just as Darla had planned, local reporters were there to talk to us about the experience. No one asked me, but if they had, I'd like to think I might have stopped giggling long enough to say something profound and practiced, like what Elizabeth Jarvis, Berks County Junior Miss, told the *Reading Times*.

"Being away from my family deepened my gratitude to them," Jarvis said. "This is a day of celebration, a very special Thanksgiving."

I never did thank my parents properly for the Junior Miss experience. And my performance that Friday and Saturday night didn't speak for me. I was out of step during the Snow White routine. When the judges asked me what I'd do to ensure world peace, I can't remember what I said, but am sure I blinked and stammered. And, when it came time for my piano solo, I started in the wrong key and bumbled to the end.

I did not win. Mary Yanochko, Miss Luzerne County, a five-foot brunette who also won both the Kraft Hostess

Award and the Simplicity Pattern scholarship, did. She told the *Reading Times* that she'd dreamed of winning the Junior Miss title since she was a child.

"I'm in shock," she said. "I don't believe it. But I guess dreams do come true."

She planned to use the scholarship money to help her reach her other dream: achieving world peace by becoming a computer systems analyst.

I did not win the Coca-Cola Spirit Award, the Physical Fitness Award, the Creative and Performing Arts Award, the Poise and Appearance Award, or the Scholastic Achievement Award. I was not a finalist. Backstage, although I didn't cry, I felt terrible, especially when my mother, in one dramatic moment of stage-mothering, grabbed hold of my shoulders and said, "You didn't even want to win."

What could I say?

By Sunday morning, it was all over. No more photographers, no more TV cameras. Even Darla had disappeared. Because my plane ticket was one-way, my parents and I packed my things—along with my Junior Miss complimentary gift pack, which included a pair of socks, a decorative can of pretzels, a box of candy, and some bulldog lapel pins courtesy of Mack Truck—and headed for my father's car, which was parked in the motel lot.

When he turned the ignition, nothing happened. He tried again. Nothing. When he opened the hood, he found that someone had stolen the battery.

"Goddamn cockroaches," he said, then hitchhiked to a nearby Sears for a replacement while my mother and I—

who, in the tradition of stage mothers and daughters everywhere, were not speaking—sat in the car.

Years later, whenever the subject of the pageant came up, my mother would say again, "You know, you didn't want to win."

Sometimes I think about what would have happened if things had turned out differently. Maybe I would have done well at Syracuse. Instead, I ended up doing just fine at a small college in Erie, Pennsylvania, which gave me four years of good scholarship money anyway. Maybe by now I would have been famous. Maybe I would have learned sooner that good work matters more than fame. Maybe my parents would have been happier.

I doubt it.

Looking back, I think I knew from that initial photo op that the pageant wasn't for me. Like I said, the first clue was that even Santa was a wreck. He seemed to enjoy his work, though, especially when he had the chance to chuckle "ho, ho, ho" as each of us came up to perch on him and ask for our Christmas wish—to be winners, or at least runners-up—while the cameras popped and rolled.

I was near the end of the line, and so by the time I made it to Santa's lap, his face glistened and there were stains under his arms. Santa smelled like an odd blend of sweat, Old Spice, and mothballs.

When I sat down and got ready to pose with my great big Junior Miss grin—which a fuchsia-lipped Darla demonstrated from her place behind one of the photographers—I noticed Santa had a hard-on.

I wasn't completely sure it was a hard-on at the time. I was seventeen, and pretty naive. After all, my parents had nearly disowned me for kissing my boyfriend. Besides, Santas, Easter Bunnies, and their assorted cronies were not supposed to get hard-ons, so this was surprising. Still, hard-on or not, whatever Santa was packing was enough to make me scooch forward until I had to balance on the edge of his right knee. Santa—maybe trying to help me balance, probably not—held my hips.

In the picture in the paper the next day, I was smiling nervously. My chin was tucked down into the ruffles on my shirt. I looked fat and insane. Still, when Darla saw the picture, she seemed pleased.

"That's what I'm talking about," she said over break-fast, handing me extra copies of the paper. "Look at that smile. A real winner."

strip yahtzee

My father, in spite-driving mode, was doing sixty in a thirty-five. Up ahead, I could see Lake Erie, the waves making puddles on the pier we were screeching toward.

"Dad, slow down," I said. "It's a dead end."

"Goddamn school has to be around here somewhere," he said. Then he ran a red light.

Along the dock were piles of what looked like dirty snow. Sure, this was Erie, Pennsylvania, the snow belt, but it was August and maybe eighty degrees. It was also freshman move-in day, 1982, at this little Catholic university where I'd decided to spend the next four years of my life.

I'd never seen the school and didn't know much about it. I'd signed up because they'd offered me a good scholarship and their course catalog listed some oddball classes in parapsychology, poetry, and silent-film studies. I applied only because the campus was within an hour's drive of my boyfriend's very nice, Ivy-League-wannabe college, where they had fancy-pants college things like trees and grass and coed dorms.

I'd given up on Syracuse after my Junior Miss debacle, and NYU was strictly out of my price range. No one in my family had gone to college, and my high school guidance counselor—an aging, leisure-suited hippie who smelled like the soy burgers the cafeteria tried to pass off as beef—wasn't much help.

After looking at my SAT scores, which showed that, where math was concerned, I had the IQ of a lunch box, he'd asked, "So what do you plan to major in?"

I said, "Journalism. I want to be a writer."

"Good," he said. "Because you can't do anything else."

I wanted to remind him that, just a month or so before, he had handed out stubby number two pencils and given my class a test—the scholastic aptitude version of *What Color Is Your Parachute?* The test revealed that I, mathematical deficiencies aside, should not be a writer. I should do something more civic-minded. According to the laminated, cartoon-illustrated test cards with their multiple-choice questions and undisclosed margins of error, I was destined to be a fireman-slash-psychologist.

Looking back, there might have been something to it. At eighteen, I already knew firsthand that salt snuffed out bacon-grease fires, that bologna was flammable, and that one should never throw water on a smoking toaster. Plus, I had read some Freud and Jung, and so I knew enough about the human psyche to diagnose my guidance counselor as an anal-retentive obsessive-compulsive who probably had issues with his mother.

My diagnosis was confirmed when, after our test was

over, he stood in front of the room and counted out loud as
we passed the pencils forward and dropped them into a box
on his desk. When he came up a few pencils short of where
he'd started, he dumped the pencils out of the box, lined
them up with all the points pointing the same way, and re-
counted, this time silently to himself, his lips moving. When
he finished and came up short again, he went ballistic.

"No one's going anywhere until I get back what's
mine, you hear?" he said when the change-of-class bell
rang. "The future of America. Ha. I don't need any aptitude test to tell me you're all liars and thieves, all of you.
Liars and thieves."

With a crackpot guidance counselor and few other
places to turn for help, I didn't know how to shop for good
schools. And my mother, who had developed a new and
odd concern for my virginity instead of my grade-point
average, wouldn't let me follow my slightly better-
informed boyfriend to the college of his choice.

At the time, my mother had been reading illustrated
manuals with titles like *The Terrible Teens*, *The Big Talk*,
and *What to Do When the Big Talk Isn't Enough*.

"All I knew about sex was, don't let a boy get on top
of you," my mother said repeatedly, usually over dinner. "I
thought you got pregnant if a boy put his tongue in your
mouth. That's how much I knew. But now things are different. Now you've got to be informed."

To be fair, my mother had just started menopause
around the same time I started my senior year in high
school. Besides, she was a nurse, so she had to know that

breasts really did sprout on their own, and not just because boys had been playing with them. So maybe it was hormones and not insanity that made her threaten to take me to a doctor to make sure I wasn't having sex.

"If you're up to what I think you're up to, you're not going anywhere. It's community college for you," she'd say. "We're not paying for you to go off and screw around with your little boyfriend."

My father, who'd disabled the locks on the bedroom and bathroom doors so that my mother couldn't lock herself in whenever a hot flash/weeping fit came on, pretty much ignored her. During our dinner talks, he'd concentrate on shoveling meat into his mashed potatoes or hand-feeding Tina II, who at this point, having been banned from her seat at the table by my mother, had taken up a more covert position between my father's knees. When forced, my father would say, "Don't upset your mother," or "Get me some milk, will you?"

One time, though, after my mother had locked herself in the car in the garage and threatened to gas it up, my father turned on me.

"You think you're so smart," he said. "Little Miss College."

"She's crazy," I said. "She needs pills. Get the shoe box."

"You know what you know? Nothing," my father said, stabbing at the food on his plate. "Smart-ass. You think you know what love is? Look what I have to live with. Christ. I could wipe my ass with what you know about love."

• • •

My father may have been right, as far as my own life was concerned. But one thing I did know was my parents' love story.

By modern standards, it would be called stalking.

My father and a navy buddy, fresh off a drinking bender that included several stolen cases of Iron City Beer, stumbled upon my mother and her nursing school cronies on a Braddock, Pennsylvania, sidewalk in October 1948.

My eighteen-year-old mother, who'd been a double-D cup as long as I'd known her, was wearing a knee-length skirt and stockings with back seams she'd drawn on with an eyebrow pencil. According to my father, although she always had great polka legs, it was my mother's tight peach turtleneck that made him swoon.

He hooted. He catcalled. He whistled. He called her toots. He dropped to the sidewalk, held his chest, and did a tongue-lolling death scene.

"She acted all high and mighty," my father said. "She turned her nose up. But she loved it."

"He wouldn't go away unless I gave him my phone number," my mother said. "I wanted him to go away."

My father, drunk or not, dangerous or not, was cute. He dressed in baggy suits, carried a comb in his pocket, and wore his hair slicked into waves. Even without a leather jacket, my father looked like a rebel in 1948, the year James Dean, with a bowl cut and glasses, played Frankenstein in his high school's production *Goon with the Wind*.

For whatever reason, when my father demanded her

number, my mother didn't add an extra digit or give him the direct line to the hospital's psychiatric ward. She gave him her real phone number, the number of the women's dorm at the Braddock Hospital School of Nursing.

My father called three times a day every day for two weeks until she agreed to go out with him.

They went dancing. They drank highballs and whiskey sours. My father got drunk and tried to cop a feel. My mother was outraged and threatened to walk home. Things went on like this for eight months. Then they got married.

"He couldn't keep his hands off me," my mother said. "He just couldn't wait."

My father never refuted this, and, as far as I can remember, even when things between them seemed awful, he always told my mother she was beautiful.

Romance aside, according to the nursing school's rules, female students weren't allowed to be married. And my mother's family didn't like my father. My grandfather, wielding an ax he used to chop chickens' heads off, had threatened him twice. My father's parents, Polish immigrants who spoke little English, didn't like my mother, either. She was Italian, didn't speak Polish, and wore bright orange lipstick. That was enough.

"She looks like a gypsy," my grandmother told my father, in Polish, after he'd brought my mother home for the first time. "Watch your pockets."

My parents were married in a civil ceremony, with a justice of the peace presiding and two civil servants as witnesses. Back in Braddock, my father rented a flat and didn't explain to his friends or family the hand-embroidered kittens and butterflies that showed up on his dish towels and pillowcases. He called it his bachelor pad, and for two years, my parents kept their first marriage secret.

When my mother graduated, they got married again, this time in a church with a fat Polish priest. They had a basement reception. Balloons and streamers draped the stair rail and support beams of my mother's childhood home, and some of the taller men had to cock their heads to avoid bumping them on the low ceiling. My mother, in her low-cut cream-colored gown, served up slices of home-made wedding cake, and both of my parents looked, in pictures, conspiratorially happy.

I'm sure that they loved each other, but, in the years I knew them, they fought. Years later, when my mother would tell me that my father, who'd just turned seventy, was sick in the head because he'd gotten a prescription for Viagra, I finally had evidence of something else I'd known all along. My parents, despite their steamy beginnings, had not had sex in a long time.

This all made my mother's obsession with my sex life odd, particularly because I wasn't having sex. My high school boyfriend, more so than me, was a Hallmark-card romantic. Translate *romantic* here to mean "virgin by choice." Sure, my boyfriend played center on the football team and had suffered his share of manly concussions, but he secretly loved fluffy kittens and Air Supply and was saving himself for marriage.

"I don't want to screw up," he said the night we fired

up a fondue pot and, because neither of us knew how to play poker, played a round of strip Yahtzee instead. His grandparents had gone out of town, and we had their house, their party games, and their polka records all to ourselves.

"We shouldn't rush things," he said, as we dry-humped post-Yahtzee in our underwear on his grandparents' scratchy tweed couch.

His own parents had been married twice, both times to each other. When he and I first started dating, his parents were on their second downswing. His father, a locally renowned history buff and Trivial Pursuit master, had his own deck-building company and tended to disappear for weeks at a time "on business." This left his mother, Donna, to ponder her freedom on her couch every night. I'm sure that watching his parents stumble their way toward a second divorce only added to my boyfriend's caution.

"It will be so much better if we wait," he'd said the one time I showed up at his house wearing a pair of fishnet stockings and a very itchy lace teddy I'd bought on the sly at Kmart.

I tried to be coy and sexy and irresistible. I'd been reading *Cosmo* and had taken its advice to use a soft-serve ice cream cone to practice French kissing. I leaned into him and tried to push my tongue seductively into his mouth, but the stockings were distracting. They kept bunching up around my ankles—partly because they were cheap and partly because I couldn't figure out how to anchor them to the little ribbon-covered snaps that dangled from the teddy.

"We're waiting until we get married," I told my mother. She didn't buy it.

She began checking the mileage on my car and standing at the door with a flashlight whenever I'd come home from a date. I wasn't sure what she could learn about my sex life from an odometer, but I knew she was checking my pupils to see if they were dilated, an obvious sign that I was destined to be not only a prostitute, but a drug addict as well.

"Don't try to pull one over on me," she'd say. "I know what you're up to."

And so sharing a college with my sweet and obstinate, abstinent boyfriend, especially a college with coed dorms, was out.

The school in Erie had a journalism program. It had writing classes. It was more than three hours away from my mother and her hormone-replacement therapy. The impending loss of my virginity was within driving distance.

I took what I could get.

As my father propelled our car closer to the pier and to what I was sure would be our Hollywood stunt dive into the lake, there was a smell that I'd come to forever associate with Erie the same way I associate rotten eggs with the sulfur creek back home.

"Are those fish dead?" my mother asked, pointing to what we could now see were piles of white and wormy carcasses cooking in the sun.

On the bad-omen scale, dead fish fall somewhere between severed horse heads and the double-cheeked kiss. But the

Corleones were pussies compared with my menopausal mother, and so unless dead fish ended up tucked between my new pink flannel sheets, I wasn't about to hightail it home.

I helped navigate for my father until we found what seemed like an entrance to a campus—one stone mansion with a postage-stamp patch of grass out front. This was Old Main, the building featured on all of the college's brochures.

In the pictures on those brochures, students were always sprawled on the grass, giving the airbrushed illusion that the campus was lush and green.

The campus was not lush and green.

Students did not sun themselves in front of Old Main. There was a sign that read KEEP OFF THE GRASS, and the grass itself had to be replanted each spring—a by-product of Erie's polar winters or the tendency of Erie-ites not to curb their dogs.

As a landmark building, though, Old Main was nice enough. It was also historically famous. Once, during a visit to Erie in the early 1900s, President William Howard Taft got stuck in a bathtub there, and his aides had to use a few pounds of butter to pry him out.

The rest of the college—half a dozen or so institutional-looking buildings and a handful of decrepit mansions that served as fraternity houses—wasn't so pretty. The best asset, as far as I could tell, was that McDonald's, a Goodwill Thrift Shop, and the police station were all within walking distance. The *Erie Daily Times* was there, too, and even though the *Times* building itself could have been mistaken for a home improvement superstore, my spirits buoyed.

"I'll get a job there," I told my parents when we flew past. "Perfect."

"A newspaper?" my father said. "I thought you wised up and were going to be on TV, like Barbara Walters. Nobody reads newspapers. They use newspapers for their dogs to piss on."

If I needed another dose of discouragement, I found it when my father, instead of mercifully plunging the car into Lake Erie, pulled up in front of the freshman dorm. Despite the big sign out front and the dozens of parents carrying milk crates full of hot pots and poufy pink comforters, I was sure there had been a mistake. The dorm—a girls-only dorm—faced a men's prison.

"It's sick," my father said. "Sickos."

"You're coming home," my mother said.

"It's fine," I said. "Don't worry."

I figured that they, whoever *they* were, wouldn't have put a prison in the middle of the city if it wasn't safe. This is the same logic I'd use a few years later when taking my new car for a spin on Daytona Beach. I was sure that *they* had strategically mapped out just how far the tide came in, and that the areas designated for driving were beyond the high-tide mark. I was sure of this right up to the moment water began seeping in through the passenger-side door.

Despite the prison's bars, some of the windows opened. On warm days, guards or prisoners—I was never sure which—would pee from four stories up and hope to get some attention. Sometimes, they'd yell things. On this particular day in late August, when my parents were helping me unload my stash of fuzzy sweaters, new underwear, and school supplies, somebody hooted "tits and ass and ass and tits" in a cheerleader rhythm, complete with hand claps.

"I give you a month, two tops," my mother said.

"We'll see each other every weekend," my boyfriend said when I called weeping on the phone later that night. "You just have to make it through the week."

"That's five days to two. Not a good deal," I said. "Did I mention my room has a great view of a guy named Bubba? We're going to be good friends. We can moon each other back and forth, you know, like Morse code."

I'd come to realize that, when it came to omens, I'd greatly underestimated the power of dead fish.

That first weekend, and nearly every weekend for months, I made what felt like my own prison break and hopped a bus at the Erie Greyhound station. Bus stations everywhere are sad and desperate places, but Erie's seemed like something out of Dante. The place was done up in traffic-cone orange and smelled, expectedly, like piss. The only amenity was a banged-up coffee machine, the kind that required exact change and squirted out something that looked like boiled tobacco spit into thin paper cups. On my first visit to the Erie station, I saw a policewoman use her billy club to beat the bare and bloated soles of a man's feet while he slept on a bench. "Get a move on," she kept shouting, but I think this had happened before because the man just lifted his head, looked at her, and then went on sleeping.

"I've got to get out of there," I'd tell my boyfriend when he'd come to pick me up in Meadville.

Meadville, Sharon Stone's hometown, is only an hour outside Erie, though it's a two-and-a-half-hour bus ride. Meteorologists often refer to it, since every few years Meadville becomes famous for being the dreariest town in the United States. Studies have claimed that Meadville residents, lacking sunshine, tend to be depressed and addicted to Internet dating. But for me, Meadville, compared with Erie, might as well have been Costa del Sol.

"I have to transfer," I'd say.

"To where?" he'd ask, and I'd shrug.

"Somewhere, anywhere, who knows," I'd say, and do nothing about it.

I was lazy and clueless, and so, instead of mapping my way out, I hunkered down and hoped things would get better. I'd make pro-and-con lists in my 8 AM religion and philosophy class, where no amount of coffee could prepare me to discuss free will, whether or not God was omnipotent or dead, or how my new tendency to drink too many mai tais and puke on my bedsheets would affect my afterlife.

I tried to make the best of it when my roommate had a breakdown, stopped going to classes, and holed up in our room, where she ate Mallo Cups and watched *The Guiding Light* and game shows all day. I didn't mind this much, since her favorite game show was *Let's Make a Deal*, which I liked, too, because there was always the chance that a football player dressed as a nun and a grand-mother dressed as a chicken might fistfight. But at night, my roommate would let the TV go to static and pace, in her floppy duck-footed way, while whistling the theme song to *Mayberry RFD*. When she would finally collapse, half dressed, onto her bed, she snored, and once she hit the REM stage, she alternately giggled and wept in her sleep.

My writing classes were my only hope. I still believed that, in spite of everything, college would be my literary gateway. I aspired not only to a job at the local paper, but to life as a real writer. I'm not sure where I got all my ideas about what constituted a real writer, because up to this point I'd never met one, but I'd guess it was the combined influence of Rod McKuen, made-for-TV movies about tem-peramental alcoholic artists and the people who love them, what I'd learned about Emily Dickinson in high school, and the pictures of writers I'd seen on book jackets.

One day, very early in my first semester, I headed for that Goodwill, just a few blocks away, with plans to culti-vate a serious writer persona.

For ten bucks, I bought an antique typewriter and my first fez. The typewriter, a shiny black Corona, came with a free bottle of dried-up Wite-Out and a pack of yellowed paper. The hat was perfect—a dark gray number with a thick black velvet band and broken-in rim that settled Humphrey-Bogart-like over my right eyebrow. I also bought a pair of black-velveteen knickers, some white men's shirts, and a few ties. The ties were polyester and skinny and reeked of cat pee, but had great style—black with hot pink polka dots, magenta stripes on fluorescent yellow, and one covered with road-sign arrows and the words I'M WITH STUPID.

"Costume party?" a woman in a crooked red wig asked as she added up my purchases on a notepad that read SMILE—GOD LOVES YOU. NO REFUNDS. NO RETURNS.

I'd go to my journalism and poetry classes looking like Hemingway's Lady Brett after a weeklong bender and sit in the front row, earning my class participation points by nodding seriously at my professors' profound insights and laughing at their jokes. Please don't think I was insincere—I truly loved these classes and the professors and believed I was, finally, learning something that seemed important.

Since life with my roommate made sleep usually impossible, I stayed up late, scribbling notes in a journal and writing teenage-angst poems I hoped would go over big with my poetry professor, a sweet blond woman and talented poet who had published some middle-aged uterus/blood/vagina-angst poems of her own in literary journals. In her poetry workshop, she had assigned some wonderful, and, for me, life-changing books like Carolyn Forché's *The Country Between Us* and Gerald Stern's *Red Coal*. She brought other real live poets to campus. Most of all, she was patient and kind when it came to ambitious, fez-wearing students like me.

"Good imagery. The way you write the tomato is vivid," she'd written on one of my early poems about two lovers, Adam and Eve, who strip naked in a suburban garden and feed each other vegetables. "The worm is phallic. Go with this."

I didn't know what phallic was and had to look it up,

but I was happy and encouraged. Out of class, I'd try to develop a taste for other literary things like whiskey and cherry cigars. I'd imagine my future—*New York Times*, Pulitzer Prize—then steal what I thought were the best lines from my late-night poems and use them in long, tear-bloated letters to my boyfriend.

In the letters, I wrote as if he were stuck on a merchant marine ship and dying of dysentery somewhere in the South Pacific. In the letters, I'd compare his lips to cotton candy, his tongue to a new puppy, his arms to bridges, his eyes to dewy sapphires. Then I'd toss a pillow at my roommate, who'd snort mid-giggle, then go back to snoring, looking pleased with herself.

Even though I didn't stay up late mastering the art of the inverted pyramid, I was pretty serious about my journalism classes as well. My journalism professor—a short, round man with a buttery laugh—wore tweed blazers and glasses and loved coffee even more than I did. He was also an editor at the *Erie Daily Times*. I was determined to make him my new best friend.

After a few weeks, when I had proven my passion for the AP Stylebook and my understanding of the difference between affect and effect, my professor had hinted that, if I did well in his class, I might be able to land a summer internship in the *Times* sports department.

"But I don't know anything about sports," I told him. "I almost failed gym."

"Don't worry about it," he said. "So did half the sportswriters."

By the end of our freshman year, I had a desk in the *Times'* sports department and something bad had happened to my sweet and athletic boyfriend. He'd become a former jock. When he didn't get a full athletic scholarship, he abandoned his football dreams. Soon he was getting his competitive fix by kicking a little frat-boy ass in Friday-night Quarters tournaments.

"It's all in the wrist," he told me, demonstrating how he could consistently land a sticky quarter in a shot glass, then throw a perfectly placed pointer elbow, which translated to "Drink, motherfucker," in one fluid motion.

"Pure skill," he said. "Nothing less."

When he learned that I'd gotten the sports internship, he was thrilled. For him, this marked not only a new phase in my would-be writing career, but a turning point in our relationship.

Now, instead of spending weekends listening to me bemoan my choice of colleges or recite romantic poems I hoped would make him turn his back on celibacy, he could lie on the couch he'd pilfered from a Dumpster, crack open a fresh bag of potato chips, and watch sports.

That's what he called it, watching sports. This general category included everything from football to miniature golf and midget wrestling. If it was on TV and, by the end, there was a winner and a loser, it qualified as serious athletic viewing.

"It's great to see you taking an interest," he said one time when we were cuddled up over a bag of Ruffles, watching two veteran fishermen square off in a Big Bass tournament. "I think this job of yours is taking us to a whole new level."

I figured this level was a particularly gruesome one, a ring of hell reserved for people who hated sports during their lifetimes. I pictured myself in the afterlife, head shoved into a leather harness by a professional wrestler named The Punisher, tennis ball duct-taped in my mouth, eyelids held open with golf tees, forced to watch competitive doggy-paddlers race across an Olympic-size pool for eternity while Pittsburgh's own Myron Cope did the play-by-play.

"Double yoi! Look at 'em go! It's dog-eat-dog out there."

It's not that I didn't try to summon up some enthusiasm during these weekend rendezvous with what I called the wild world of sports. I liked potato chips, and tried to think of our weekend couch sessions as both intimacy and homework. After all, as long as I didn't block the TV or his chip access, my boyfriend was content to snuggle for hours at a time. Homework-wise, I didn't want to let my good professor down and knew I needed help deciphering my new beat.

Once, when my boyfriend and I were watching a Lakers–Celtics game, I cheered as Kareem Abdul-Jabbar scraped himself up off the floor after a particularly vicious foul.

"What a great rebound!" I said, feeling very proud.

"What the hell's wrong with you?" my boyfriend said. Maybe even then I knew we were never meant to be.

Still, if there was one thing my life in sports taught me,

it's how to throw a cliché. Quitters never win, and, where my love life was concerned, I had heart. I wasn't about to lose my first real chance as a writer, either. And besides, I was young and still prone to romantic idealism. So I forced myself to give 100 percent where my boyfriend and my sportswriting assignments were concerned.

When I was sent out to interview Karl Klepfer, a mountain climber whose specialty was scaling glaciers, I did some hands-on research by hiking up one of the ice dunes that sprouted on Lake Erie every winter. Alone on top of the dune, bundled up in a hot pink down parka and furry mittens, I felt very poetic, and wished I had a notebook in which I could scribble down my thoughts as I witnessed a dramatic sunset over the beautiful, frozen lake. It looked like pictures of Antarctica I'd seen in *National Geographic*, and the experience felt that exotic and faraway.

Later, I'd learn that ice dunes are hollow and every winter in Erie, at least one poor idiot dies by falling into one. But Karl Klepfer, who himself climbed ice dunes for fun—albeit with ropes and other assorted gear—understood what had propelled me. And I got a pretty good interview.

"When I go out, there's nothing I dread," he told me. "I think of the sunsets and the sunrise and what they look like out over the ice. There's something the ice does to them. It makes them shine. It's really beautiful."

"It's like I'm writing poems, but getting paid for it," I told my boyfriend. "This might be working out after all."

"Do you think you'll get to do anything good, like Steelers preseason or anything?" he said.

What can you do?

I was in love, whatever that was.

A few weeks after I interviewed Klepfer, I was sent back on the lake, this time to talk to the fishermen who set up little tents and drilled holes through the thick ice and cast line after line, waiting, I supposed, for that one big bite. At night, you could see the fires they kept burning in steel drums, like stars all over the surface of the lake.

I figured the hours I spent with my boyfriend watching those Big Bass competitions would finally be helpful. But as beautiful as the ice-fishing camps looked at night, when I stepped off the pier, a full winter's sun was blaring down. The ice creaked and cracked with each step. I was sure I would break through at any minute.

So this was how it would end, I thought—me, crashing through ice, reporter's notebook in hand, where I'd bob around until I froze up like one of those flies in the gag ice cubes my boyfriend bought at Spencer's Gifts. I'd die covering some stupid story about lunatics who go fishing on a frozen lake in the middle of a winter cold enough to freeze nose hair.

We all have moments when we reevaluate our lives, when we wonder just how far we've veered off course, when we make deals with the universe that, should we live through this, we will be better people, more focused, grateful. For me, this was one of those moments. If I got out of this, I would seize the day. I would break up with my boyfriend. I would transfer to a better school. I'd be kinder to my parents. I'd stop screwing around.

When I made it to the first tent, relieved to have gotten that far, Gary, a veteran ice fisher in his late forties, was manning his hole. Three fishing poles were anchored in the ice, their lines extending deep into the water beneath our feet. Gary was big and hairy, with thick eyebrows and a scraggly graying beard. He was dressed entirely in Day-Glo orange and reminded me of a fat road-construction cone. He'd been drinking beer, and little yellowish chunks had formed in his beard and mustache. He offered me a beer, which, despite the little I knew about journalistic ethics, I took.

"Catching anything?" I asked him.

"A fucking cold," he said.

"I mean fish," I said.

"Look, sweetheart, the fishing's a front," he said. "What do you think I'd do with a fish here anyway? Eat it? You've got to be kidding. Have you seen what comes out of this lake? I'm just out here to get away from my wife and kids. I come out here to drink beer and be alone and not have to talk. The wife, she always wants to talk—feelings this and that. It's all bullshit. As for the fishing, one guy I know caught a fish with two heads here last winter. Eat these fish? You'd have to be an idiot. You'd have to be crazy. Put that in your paper. You've got to be crazy to do this, that's all."

I drank Gary's beer, took some notes, and slowly made my way back to land. By the time I climbed up the pier and hit solid ground, I'd forgotten my pact with the universe. I had a deadline. And all I could think about were Gary's words—"You've got to be crazy to do this"—and how he said I should put that in the paper.

I was.

I did.

my own personal
deep throat

When the phone rang at my desk in the newsroom, I answered the way I'd been forced to answer all month.

"*Erie Daily Times*. Love is in the air. Tell us *your* love story."

"Hello? Hello? Is this the girl? The girl who writes the stories?"

The woman was old. She was loud. This was not unusual.

Most of the calls I or any of us got were from older people who wanted to complain or get someone to do a story about their toilet-trained cats, their baton-twirling granddaughters, or their Elvis dinner plate collections.

Sometimes they wanted to give anonymous tips. During my short stint at the paper, I'd already acquired my own personal Deep Throat. Deep Throat disguised his naturally arthritic voice by slipping in and out of falsetto, which made him sound like Dolly Parton on steroids.

According to Deep Throat, local ambulance drivers

were sadistically slow. They stopped for yellow lights and refused to pass garbage trucks because they wanted old people to die before they got to the hospital. This saved money for the insurance companies.

"It's a conspiracy," Deep Throat told me. "They're in cahoots."

The local grocery clerks were also in cahoots, and were making a mint by overcharging senior citizens and the blind for lettuce and Tucks Pads. Deep Throat knew. He had receipts. One smart-ass clerk consistently overcharged him ten cents for the lettuce, fifteen cents for the pads.

"That's twenty-five cents a week," he said. "If they do that to everybody, they're home free. They think we don't know. Oh, we know all right. We know."

Like Deep Throat, most of our callers were regulars. Many of them seemed lonely. So I wasn't surprised that this woman's voice sounded familiar, though I couldn't place it at first. I spoke loud and slow, the way I talked to people who didn't speak English.

"You mean the love stories?" I said. "Yes, I'm the one."

"Oh, you're the one?" the woman said, her voice louder now, the syllables more distinct. "You're the one, all right. I hope you're proud of yourself. I'm going to sue."

For an entire month, I'd been on the love-story beat, an idea dreamed up by Pat, my latest editor. Since the summer of my freshman year in college, I'd been working my way through the *Times*' newsroom. During my internship in sports, I'd learned the valuable art of interviewing people even when I had no idea what I was interviewing them about. As a sportswriter, I modeled all my questions on *The Wide World of Sports*, the 1970s TV show with the spectacular opening shot of a skier plummeting down a mountain, legs akimbo, ski poles flailing, as he headed for the ground, neck-first, in the agony of defeat.

"Can you talk about what a thrill your victory was?" I'd ask.

"What an agonizing defeat. How do you feel?"

I got a reputation as a pretty good woman sportswriter, and stayed on in the department as a stringer for another year. Then I did a brief stint on the news desk, where I wrote obits, helped tally election results, and manned the phone line readers called whenever they wanted to complain.

Although I almost liked the sports beat, the news desk was terrible, so I thought I'd hit it big when Pat, the features editor, asked me to switch to her section.

"What do you want to write about dead people for?" she said. "Come over to the Living section, for Christ's sake. You'll get more inches, better clips."

I had the feeling that this was a standard line Pat used to swipe stringers away from other departments, but I still jumped. I wanted more inches. I wanted better clips. I had ambitions.

Next thing I knew, I was on the misery beat.

If you were blind, deaf, mute, poor, downtrodden, or ancient, and you were even the slightest bit newsworthy and lived or worked in our coverage area, chances are, during the year I spent in features, I wrote your story. I did stories on a deaf hairdresser; a one-legged farmer; two brothers—blind since birth—whose law firm's motto was "Justice Is Blind"; a paraplegic golfer; a paraplegic marathon racer; and one centenarian who'd survived slavery but blamed all evil on airplanes, televisions, and sugared breakfast cereals.

I always wrote the stories the same way. I'd lead with narrative and description, quote in the second paragraph, and then, in paragraph three, plunk down the kicker.

"And [insert subject] is [insert misery]."

After a while, I became callous. I didn't want to do stories about people who were only missing a leg or an arm. Eventually, unless you'd lost all five senses, both arms and legs, and spent your life bobbing in a jar of formaldehyde, I wasn't interested.

"I think I'd like to do something different," I told Pat. And so she hit me with the love stories.

Pat dressed like an off-duty nun and reminded me of an owl with cataracts whenever she eyeballed me through her round, thick-lensed glasses. Asexual and probably loveless, Pat swore that love, coupled with the usual stories about drug busts and drunk politicians, was all we'd need to rake in readers and advertisers.

"They love that human-interest crap," she said. "Get on it."

When I first started in features, before I was beaten down by all the misery fit to print, I adored Pat. Despite her surface unpleasantness and her fondness for oversize taupe accessories, she'd once been an editor at *Newsday* in New York.

I didn't question what an editor from New York was doing in this city of cheap chicken wings and dead fish. I thought her gruffness, her long strands of golf-ball-size taupe beads, her shapeless black suits and Franciscan monk haircut were all wonderful and worldly, and for a while I imitated her. I cut my hair and began speaking in quick, clipped sentences. I got a pair of black-framed glasses. I practiced not blinking and became addicted to Visine. And although I could never stand taupe and all other supposed earth tones never found in nature, I did start wearing black turtlenecks, even in the lakefront summer, when the humidity was 100 percent.

But now, Pat's morose, tough editor bit was getting to me, and so was the love-story beat. These love stories were happy little tales of love gone right, something I knew nothing about. But if you didn't guess this already from my sportswriting past, here's a tip: When it comes to newspapers, the people who know the least about a subject are almost always the ones assigned to cover it. If you don't read books, you're destined to be a book critic. If you have acid reflux, you'll make a great food writer. I was twenty-one years old and already horrific when it came to love. But as far as the *Erie Daily Times* was concerned, I was the resident expert on romance.

By this time, things with my boyfriend were ending ugly, the way such things usually do. We still commuted to each other's colleges most weekends, and still said "No, you first" whenever we had to hang up the phone during late-night calls. We were also engaged. I had a ring—a lovely little pear-shaped sliver—by the time we finally had sex at the Cloverleaf Motel on Christmas break our junior year.

The Cloverleaf, a by-the-hour dive back home, offered free cable and a romantic view of the traffic on Route 30. Our room came complete with cigarette burns on the bedspread, a painting of cowboys slaughtering a herd of buffalo over the bed, and carpeting that was mysteriously sticky. But the bed was hooked up to a Magic Fingers massager, and we spent an entire roll of quarters on foreplay. I'd brought candles and a lacy, highly flammable polyester nightgown-and-robe set that I'd sprayed with fake designer cologne.

"It's called a peignoir," I said, having looked up both the word and the pronunciation beforehand. "Like it?" I rolled around on the limp mattress and struck a Madonna "Like a Virgin" pose.

"It's nice," my now-fiancé said. "What's that smell?"

As for him, he wore his laundry-day tighty-whiteys, the ones with tiny moth holes in the butt, and brought plastic-wrapped roses and a bottle of Riunite, which we chilled in the motel ice bucket and drank from the complimentary sanitary-wrapped cups.

Despite our efforts at storybook romance, the sex was quick and scary and afterward we took turns locking ourselves in the bathroom.

I'm not saying sex was the only thing that went wrong. After all, we were young and, speaking for myself, full of the drama TV specials are made of. But it started to seem that not having sex—and all the talking and vowing and bad letter-writing that involved—was what had kept us together all along. Once we had sex, we didn't have much to talk about.

I noticed this right after we turned in the motel room key.

"So," I said.

"So?" he said.

"So," I said, and tossed my purse into the backseat of his Nova. My purse was bulging with the sheet I'd stolen from the bed like it was a crime scene. I'd been too embarrassed to leave the sheet for the housekeepers to find, though I didn't have a plan for how to get rid of it. Somehow, my boyfriend had thought this through, and he pulled over at a nearby McDonald's, where I chucked both the sheet and the peignoir into a Dumpster.

We didn't say anything more until he dropped me off at my parents' house.

"So?" he said.

"So," I said, and kissed him, missing his lips and hitting his cheek instead.

Over the next year or so, we experimented with edible underwear, furry handcuffs, and cinnamon-flavored self-heating lotions we'd buy at Spencer's Gifts. But I started to notice his bad hygiene. His teeth were often sticky with plaque and his breath smelled like salami. He started to notice that my thighs were disproportionately large when compared with my breasts.

Once, when we were at the beach in Erie, he said I should go back to wearing one-piece bathing suits.

"That makes you look, I don't know, weird," he said, pulling at the strings of my white string bikini. "Sort of like someone inflated your butt."

The magic was gone.

Sure, he still told me that whenever he heard "Hungry Like the Wolf," he thought of me bobbing naked on the flubbery water bed he'd bought at a garage sale, even though water beds, especially leaky ones, were prohibited in his lease. I told him that I'd always thought of Billy Joel's "Vienna" as our song, with its love-and-wanderlust themes and all, and said I couldn't wait for us to be married and move to Florida—his dream destination and the one thing that he and my father could talk about. There, in the Sunshine State, we'd live happily ever after, with our industrial air conditioner, our screened-in porch, an endless supply of gin and grapefruit juice, and an MTV-inspired sex life, complete with body oil and ice cubes.

I didn't know about Duran Duran's actual effect on my fiancé's libido, but I already knew that (a) I wasn't ready to get married; (b) I'd rather move to a trailer park in Ohio and be eaten by squirrels than live in Florida year-round; (c) gin and grapefruit juice make me puke; and (d) no matter how hard we tried, the sex just wasn't like anything I'd seen on TV.

What can I say? In between our weekend visits, he developed a crush on a redhead who didn't shave her legs or armpits, and I'd started falling for writer-artist types. For me, writer-artist types included a bucktoothed newspaper editor; a science-fiction writer who loved Civil War reenactments and thought showing me how to make my own bullets was romantic; and a drinking buddy who loved Hemingway as much as I did and dreamed of living on a houseboat off the coast of Cuba.

In our small-town ways, we were, I suppose, becoming worldly. In the end, there would be more first-love drama—lacy underwear and my prized Hemingway books hurled out of windows; one incident involving aspirin and a bottle of cheap and luckily vomit-inducing vodka; several cases of breaking and entering; one drunk-and-disorderly arrest; and plenty of all-out weeping. But when his mother finally called to ask for the engagement ring back, I sent it to her. And that was that.

At the paper, people would send in their love-story ideas on forms like the ones we used for obituaries. Each week, Pat would go through them and pick the one or two she thought stood out. She'd hunt for tales that mixed the finer points of the misery beat with this one.

Most of the stories Pat picked featured lucky-in-love couples where at least one of the lovers met misery-beat criteria. If the lovers started their day helping each other strap on artificial limbs, terrific. And if the lovers were holding hands through their retirement years, Pat saw demographic stars.

"Here's one with double the human-interest crap!" she'd say, and toss a form on my desk.

As far as I could tell, Pat was right. Golden-aged romance made for a direct hit with our paper's largest group of subscribers, who were mostly in their sixties and, like Deep Throat, were also the ones with the most time to write letters to the editor, wander by the newsroom, or call in bomb threats.

Usually, readers loved the love stories, as Pat predicted, so the calls were almost always positive. I couldn't imagine what I'd done to the woman on the phone to warrant a lawsuit.

"This is Alice Clapper," she said. "You might remember me."

I'd done a story on Alice Clapper and her husband, Fred. The story had run the day before. The gist of it was that Fred was the oldest man alive in McKean, a small town outside Erie. Alice's sister, Bertha, was the town's oldest woman. Alice was eighty-seven. Fred was ninety-one. They'd been married for nearly sixty years. The story I wrote was unremarkable, if you leave out the parts about Alice's brother being killed by a pitchfork and Fred's climbing a mountain in Brazil when he was seventy-five.

Both Fred and Alice were kind people who, give or take a moment, were still pretty sharp. They both had all their limbs and knew who was president. I'd been in their house, the same one Fred was born in back in 1895. Alice, her white hair curled and teased and sprayed until it looked like dollops of whipped cream on her head, was a good hostess. She made tea and showed off her photograph albums. I took notes. A photographer snapped a picture. Eight hundred words later, I thought my work was done.

"You've ruined me," she said. "I can't show my face at church. My daughter can't go to card club. I'm finished."

I thought Alice was upset that I'd quoted Fred saying, "One day she just conned me into marrying her," or, since I knew she was the church type, that I'd let him swear twice in print: one *hell* ("War was hell, but I had fun"— Fred on World War I) and one *damn* ("It's a damn shame"—Fred on poverty in his hometown).

But it turned out she had no problem with Fred's tendency to cuss. The problem, she said, was the following sentence: "The gray house, which sits facing Main Street, is sparsely but cozily furnished, with calico cushions and dusty antiques."

"Dust? Dust?" Alice said, her voice going up in pitch until she sounded like Deep Throat doing his falsetto. "I'll have you know I'm an excellent housekeeper. I might be old, but I keep things neat. There is no dust in my house."

I tried to interrupt, tried to say I'd seen what I'd seen, but Alice wasn't having it.

"People think because they read something in the paper it's true. They don't know. You're writing fiction at that paper, that's what you're doing. Love story? Ha. What do you know? Fiction, I tell you. *National Enquirer*."

Instead of pressing it, I just apologized and offered to run a correction, though I wasn't quite sure how I'd word one. "There is no dust on Alice Clapper's antiques. The *Times* regrets the error."

"Never mind. Your sorry is good enough. I hope you learned something from this, young lady," Alice said. "I hope you learned something."

i'm into leather

Although I've always loved the Ramones, I was twenty-six before I ever owned a leather jacket. It was a gift from my friend Christian, who was tired of me whining about the graduate poetry workshop I was taking at the University of Pittsburgh.

After I'd finished undergraduate school, I'd stuck around the *Erie Daily Times* as a stringer. Finally, after being worn down by calls from people like Alice Clapper and Deep Throat, not to mention one final features assignment where I was sent camping with the Girl Scouts and ended up nearly getting sucked into a tornado, I did a short stint in public relations at another Erie college. There, I met Diana, another wild-haired poetry professor, who suggested that I give grad school a try.

"It will buy you some time to write," she said. "You know, until you figure out what it is you're doing."

Until I met Diana, I didn't know that people actually got master's degrees, even doctorates, in poetry. It sounded perfect. Seven months later, I was back home in

Pittsburgh, on a scholarship, working toward a master of fine arts degree at Pitt.

An MFA in poetry, by the way, as everyone in my family was happy to point out, is a very practical degree.

"At least you'll be able to write something good on those signs you'll be holding up," one of my cousins said. "Will Rhyme for Food."

Around the time Christian gave me the leather jacket, I had been writing some sappy (I would have said authentic) but distinctively rhyme-free (I would have said organic) working-class poems, and one snotty professor had been giving me a hard time.

"She said my poems lacked meaning and emotion," I said, pretending to peer over invisible bifocals and summoning up my best British accent, even though the prof in question was from Nevada and did not at that time wear glasses.

Christian and I were sulking over warm beers at Chiefs, a hipster-dufus dive in North Oakland that catered to aging hipster-dufusses like us.

A hard-core slam poet, Christian had performed at Lollapalooza and the Nuyorican Cafe in New York. He had street cred, not to mention serious dreadlocks that shot out of his head like spikes. I'd had a few poems published in obscure journals with names like *Poem* and *West Branch*, and was into black turtlenecks, black jeans, and my tragic, trademark pair of purple hightop Chuck Taylors.

"I know one guy. He brought a bowie knife to one of those workshops once," Christian said, ripping the label off a bottle of Iron City and adding it to the pile of metallic shreds in front of him. "He didn't say anything. Just plopped the knife down on the table, gave it a little twirl, you know, like spin the bottle, and that was that. Nobody said anything to him for the rest of the semester."

"Security would have me arrested," I said. "Besides, I'm not the bowie-knife type. Everyone knows I like tofu."

That's when Christian took off his jacket.

"Here," he said. "At least wear this. You'll look tough if you lose that secretary hair."

Although it would take awhile for me to give up on perms, the jacket felt instantly right. So maybe the leather was still a little squeaky, the silver studs on the collar a bit too flashy. And maybe Christian, even though he was several inches shorter than me, was a bit too authentically violent. And sure, I probably looked ridiculous, there in the pink neon lights of this hipster bar, dressed up like the Fonz. Still, when I slipped on that jacket, I felt, maybe for the first time, completely comfortable.

When are people too old to reinvent themselves?

I spent most of my teens and early twenties trying to channel Molly Ringwald. I wanted to be the pretty arty/cheerleader type—sweet, popular—and tried hard to fight my natural-born angst.

This explains not only my Junior Miss debacle, but also why I joined the marching band at Penn Trafford High School, where I would go down in history as the worst majorette ever. Once, I knocked myself out with my own baton. Another time I caused the tubas and the drum line to collide during the climax to "Night on Bald Mountain." And once, while trying to twirl fire, I singed off one of my eyebrows.

I had, of course, a motive. Although I didn't know it then, I spent most of my early years the way a lot of people do—trying, with often terrifying results, to please parents. I think that my parents, despite my less-than-auspicious beginnings, had that common hope that a perfect child could save their less-than-perfect marriage. Like I said, my mother was oddly proud of my second-place finish in that Sears beautiful-baby contest, and I think she hoped my charms would reap a lifetime supply of steak knives, family unity, and neighborhood praise.

I kept up a good front through college. Then, when I was finally sure I'd never have to spend even a weekend in my parents' house, I came loose.

I realized this one morning when I woke up in my apartment on Pittsburgh's South Side with a Carlo Rossi Vin Rosé hangover, a bad case of whiplash, and a bass player named Bix in bed beside me.

Bix was naked. I was wearing his Nirvana T-shirt. There were brown crumbs all over the sheets and in Bix's scraggly chest hair. I had a vague memory of Bix, already deeply drunk and stoned, slipping a tab of cartoon-Santa acid on his tongue, then making gingerbread from a box and feeding it to me with his fingers. The whiplash, I fig-ured, was from the dancing I'd done the night before, when Bix's band played at a club called The Electric Banana and did some rocking covers of 1970s staples like "I Got You, Babe" and "Kung Fu Fighting."

Bix was the latest in my series of romantic missteps. I'd been dating only musicians and artists, who, despite their pesky drug problems and conversational difficulties, always had nice hair. I think I'd inherited my mother's belief that hair was important.

In other words, I didn't fully embrace adolescence until I was a quarter century old.

This particular morning, Bix's hair was splayed out on two pillows. By the time he woke up, it was well past noon, which meant he was late. Once again, he was going to have to explain to his live-in girlfriend—whom he swore he hadn't had sex with in three years—where he'd been.

This kind of stress posed a problem, because it meant Bix could not brush his hair, which would make him instantly suspicious. Bix had alopecia, an unfortunate disease for a rock musician and a cheat. Whenever Bix was stressed out, his hair, which he loved even more than I did, would fall out in clumps. And so this morning, he tenderly rolled the tangled mess of long brown curls into a knit cap. He scooped out the one remaining hunk of gingerbread in the pan he'd found under the bed, and said in his swollen-tongued, phlegm-throated, romantic way, "Let's hang out later."

If there was one moment I could point to and say this is when I started to reevaluate my life, I'd like to say this was it, but it wasn't. It would take more, almost a year more, for me to realize that I was, from all angles, pretty pathetic.

I'd met Bix and other guys like him through my best friend, Trish. This was not the same Trish as the Tish from my Girl Scout Troop 18 days, but she was equally talented.

Bix was not Trish's fault, nor did she approve of my taste in men. They were simply a by-product of the world she and I ended up in.

Trish smoked Salem Slim Lights and twirled them movie-star-style between her tiny red-tipped fingers. She read Tarot cards. She knew her way around liquid black eyeliner. She drank too much and wore low-rise jeans and lacy black bra tops long before Britney Spears came on the scene. She was wonderful.

Trish was also an amazing painter, but her boyfriend Ed headed up the band Bix eventually joined. The band was called the Frampton Brothers, and Ed, a genetic splice of Peter Frampton and Kenny G, was the perfect front man.

The year I'd met Trish, she'd given up on painting, mostly because Ed didn't like the paintings she'd done of past boyfriends. Besides, Trish didn't have much time to paint, since she kept busy designing CD covers and posters for Ed's band.

Trish was happy to help out. She chose to help out. It wasn't any of my business what she did or did not do with her art. Still, I worried about her beautiful paintings wrapped up in garbage bags in the attic or hidden behind the sofa. She and I would blow all our laundry quarters playing the Ramones on a jukebox or playing pool at

Jack's Bar and we'd talk about this. She had plans—to get a better job, and then get a nicer apartment, one where she could have a studio just big enough for her easel and paints, not a guitar or amp in sight.

"This is just for now," she'd say. "There's just so much happening for Ed. I think he could really be something."

Keep in mind that I was a hypocrite, a musician posing as a groupie, a writer undercover among songwriters. Plus, even though I wished things were different for my friend, I loved Ed's band. I could understand why their single, "Dwarf Bowling," was a hit in both Japan and Germany. And I was sleeping with the bass player, after all. Despite everything, I agreed with both Trish and critics who said Ed might be the next big thing out of Pittsburgh.

Which is why I went along for the seven-hour drive to Hoboken, New Jersey, for the band's biggest CD-release party ever. The party marked the launch of *Bonograph: Sonny Gets His Share*, a compilation album featuring hip bands covering Sonny Bono's greatest hits like "Bang Bang (My Baby Shot Me Down)" and "Pammie's on a Bummer." *Bonograph* was Ed's idea, and featured R.E.M.'s touring guitarist Peter Holsapple, the Flat Duo Jets, and, of course, the Frampton Brothers. The project had been featured on MTV and CNN. It made *People* magazine.

This was big.

And so, Trish and I loaded up her paneled station wagon with plastic cups and screw-top gallons of Carlo Rossi, and toasted what we were certain would be Ed's gateway to superstardom.

When we got to Maxwell's, a nightclub smack in the middle of Frank Sinatra's old neighborhood, many of the *Bonograph* stars, including Holsapple, were on hand to celebrate. And, the rumor was, scouts from at least one major label were somewhere in the crowd.

The air probably crackled with feedback and possibility, and, at least for all those hours on the road, Trish and I had intended to share the excitement. But habit took over, and now I realize I don't remember much about that show. Like I said, Trish and I had brought along jugs of wine and, once inside the club, we commandeered two prime bar stools, an ashtray, and a fresh basket of peanuts. We didn't move except for the occasional bathroom run.

I don't remember seeing the Framptons, or any of the other acts. Turns out, although I really was a fan—I listened to the demo of the band's first album, *I Am Curious (George)*, in my car until the tape wore out—I was not a very good groupie.

I do know that, for the whole night, Trish and I were deep in conversation, probably our usual one, about how we imagined our lives would end up. We'd make it out of Pittsburgh and get cars that wouldn't break down. I'd write, she'd paint, Ed would play his music, Bix would go into rehab, I'd find a nice semi-drug-free guy, and we'd all move to New York, hang out in cafés, and be happy.

At one point, a man with a ragged Beatles haircut and nice eyes leaned between us and said, "You two are so serious. Smile, already!"

I have always hated people who tell me to smile. They

seem pushy, and an order is, after all, a horrible pickup line. But this man seemed kind. Besides, he had a Polaroid camera. I love Polaroids, all that instant gratification. And so Trish and I leaned together, both of us in our leather jackets, playing it up. Trish wore her biker hat. My blond hair was now cut short and slicked back, as far from secretary as I could get.

We tried to look cool, tough, pursing our red lips and mugging for the camera. But we couldn't hold out. Eventually, we beamed and the camera snapped, and there we were, full of sweet cheap wine and joy in that dark and beautiful club.

We didn't know that the guy with the camera was famous. We'd learn later, from the bartender, that the man was Peter Buck from R.E.M.

Years later, Ed would say we're crazy, that it was probably Peter Holsapple instead, but I've looked at pictures of Peter Buck, and this is the man I remember.

Back at Maxwell's, he'd seemed too normal, too sweet to be famous. He'd told us he was going down the block for a slice of pizza and asked us if we wanted him to bring some back. Trish and I thought he seemed like a neighborhood guy, about as far from a rock star as you could get.

But really, what did we know?

We didn't know, for instance, that I'd be the one to end up in New York. I'd work on an airplane. It would not be glamorous, though I'd keep publishing poems in little magazines no one would read.

We didn't know that, years later, nice Peter Buck

would be arrested for getting drunk on an airplane and throwing yogurt at flight attendants like me.

We didn't know that Ed would, in fact, end up famous, but more as a Pittsburgh music critic than as a musician.

We didn't know that Trish would never get back to painting, although, after she married Ed, she'd continue to stockpile paints on the sly.

We could have guessed that Bix would be a balding rehab dropout and would simply disappear. But we didn't know that Christian would make it to Europe, where he was sure he could become a famous performance poet.

"They take art seriously over there," he'd told me before he left. "Their poets are like fucking rock stars."

When things didn't work out, we didn't know that Christian would kill himself, overdosing on insulin.

He'd call me first, collect, and years later I wouldn't remember anything he said.

Maybe it would explain some things if I could remember. Probably not. None of us knew much about anything, let alone ourselves, back then.

miss new york

has everything

"While she waits impatiently for the world to recognize her talents, she takes odd jobs, copes with parents who don't always understand her, rushes from one audition to another, and has the time of her life."

—*TV Guide*'s 1966 Fall Preview Issue
introducing ABC's new sitcom *That Girl*

I blame Marlo Thomas.

Ever since I can remember, I've been obsessed with New York City. It's where people go to become famous. It's where they go to fall in love. It's the city with twenty-four-hour delis, the Brooklyn Bridge, and bagels that could double as shotputs. In New York, everyone is an artist. Everyone wears all black, all the time. They hang around cafés. In New York, even the pigeons are beautiful.

This is what I believed.

Because of Marlo.

Before Samantha bewitched Darrin, before Sally Field took off as the Flying Nun, before Maude donned her first muumuu, Marlo Thomas was That Girl.

Back in 1966, when I was an impressionable terrible two, Marlo Thomas—aka Ann Marie, lovely former meter maid who left her parents' home in Brewster to make it big in the Big Apple—was getting three thousand fan letters a week.

"I knew I was doing something important when the letters started coming in, most of them from young girls, saying, 'Because of you, I'm going to move to the big city,'" Thomas once told the *Ventura County Star.*

Between the ages of two and seven, I wasn't much of a letter writer. But during *That Girl*'s five-year run from 1966 until 1971, I gathered an impressive collection of *That Girl* coloring books, *That Girl* Colorforms, *That Girl* lunch boxes, and *That Girl* paper dolls, complete with mod wardrobes and the ubiquitous paper boyfriend Donald.

My mother made me clothes—little velvet miniskirts and sparkly gold pants—from McCall's "Marlo's Corner" collection. I wept and pleaded until my parents bought me a tiny pair of white go-go boots—specially made to fit my skinny calves—and fuchsia flower-printed tights.

From the debut show until the finale, my mother swears I didn't miss an episode. And then there were years of reruns.

Of course I was in love—with Ann Marie and her gorgeous Breck-do hair, her huge collection of sunglasses and snaptop handbags, but even more with the image of her smiling face superimposed over New York City, the Empire State Building peeping out from the bridge of her nose, Park Avenue at her lips. Ann Marie was, as the theme song said, complex. She was popcorn and white wine. She was diamonds and daisies. But more important, she was New York City, a place as exotic and impossible as Oz.

When I think about how I ended up working as a flight attendant and living on those little foil-wrapped packs of peanuts, I blame *That Girl*, and Sam Denoff's subliminal lyrics.

What every girl should be. Beautiful. Independent. A snappy dresser. Urban. Worldly. Happy.

During *That Girl*'s five seasons and afterward, I knew I would be happy only in New York. I already hated my hometown—fifteen miles from the epicenter of Pittsburgh— with its greasy fish fries and gun bashes at the bingo hall, legions of unhappy housewives in pastel-flowered housecoats, satanically peppy Girl Scouts and Up With Peoplers and endless macramé-craft marathons.

Everyone I knew thought artists were bums. No one read books or went to museums unless there was a class field trip, and then it would be mostly to see the Carnegie's T. rex or famous diorama—cavemen, who looked like the mill workers who stumbled out of Trafford's Seventh Street Tavern on payday, chasing and killing a mangy sabertooth in a papier-mâché landscape.

By the time I made it to high school, I had it all mapped out. I'd kiss Pittsburgh good-bye. I'd head for college in New York, where my life would suddenly be as glamorous as Ann Marie's. I'd given up on music during my sophomore year when I realized I was stuck at the local public high school and not Juilliard, and so I'd decided to focus on writing. I abandoned the rainbow-and-kittens motifs of my Rod McKuen days and became serious.

I read Dorothy Parker, and decided I would become a famous New York writer. My first book would be steeped in irony and pity. It would be snapped up by a big-time publisher by the time I turned twenty-one. I'd get invited to parties at Elaine's. I'd have a designer wardrobe. I'd be in *People* magazine. I was obsessed with *People* magazine. I'd have a few delightfully dumbfounded boyfriends, not unlike Donald, who'd constantly propose. I'd say, *aren't you lovely*. I'd say, *oh, Donald*. I'd say, *no thanks, I need my space.*

In the last season of *That Girl*, Donald proposes to Ann Marie, but they never get around to the marriage, because "girls don't need another married role model," Thomas said.

The last episode shows Ann and Donald on their way to a women's lib meeting. They get stuck in an elevator and their lives flash before their eyes. This life-flashing is something that happened often on the show. In Episode 104, "Fly by Night," for instance, Russell Johnson, the Professor on *Gilligan's Island*, flies Ann and Donald to her father's cabin in Vermont, but the plane runs out of gas.

They make an emergency landing, and Ann sees her life flash before her eyes.

Well, these things happen.

The next thing I knew, I was thirty, single, still in Pittsburgh. I had a master's degree in poetry, but no book. I was too exhausted to write because I was teaching part time at three different universities and spending my weekends drinking Iron City, hanging out with local bands, sleeping with musicians and artists I didn't really like, and wondering where I went wrong.

And so, one morning, as I scanned the *Pittsburgh Post-Gazette* for my horoscope, I came to the ad:

LIKE TO TRAVEL?
WANT TO MOVE TO NEW YORK?

And so of course I tore it out. *This*, I thought, *is finally it.*

I can't remember what ultimately prompted Ann Marie to ditch Brewster, but Marlo Thomas, who was also the show's uncredited executive producer, once talked about how she admired her character's devotion to her own bliss.

"I liked that she was a girl with a dream, that she was living her dream," Thomas said.

Ann Marie's dream was, of course, to become a famous actress. But she screwed up most of her gigs. In Episode 102, "Opening Night," she dreams of getting bad reviews from theater critics. The night before the opening, she gets her finger stuck in a faucet. No one hears her cries for help.

While playing a corpse on live TV, Ann Marie opens her eyes.

"No matter what, she was unstoppable," Thomas said. "She had heart."

In smaller print, the newspaper ad read:

```
Seeking smiling men and women
for world-class careers as flight
attendants.
```

For the record, I have always been afraid to fly. I once took a train—coach, not sleeper—from Pittsburgh to Florida, twenty-eight upright hours, for this very reason. I don't know why I didn't think of that when I read the ad's small print, but I didn't. Instead, I focused on the words:

"Want to move to New York?"

All of my old dreams rewound and played back. There I am, reading Kafka in Central Park. There I am, listening to Woody Allen play the clarinet at a smoky club in the Village.

But *flight attendant*?

When Ann Marie wasn't following her dream, or paying her rent and clothing bills out of her father's or Donald's wallets, she worked odd jobs. She was a door-to-door shoe salesperson, a waitress, a perfume clerk. In Episode 87, "Nobody Here but Us Chickens," she is the spokesperson for a fast-food franchise, Chicken Big. She wears a chicken suit and her legs look perfect and sexy in orange and yellow feather-printed tights.

Feathered or not, Ann Marie was irresistible to men.

One night, as he's giving her a ride home, Slim Pickens, her Chicken Big boss, makes a pass. She gets out of his car and is left alone at night on a dark country road in her chicken suit.

Her life flashes before her eyes.

Well, I reasoned, flight-attendant uniforms are nicer than fast-food getups, glamorous, even, in an old-time-movie kind of way. Plus, I'd waited tables on and off for eighteen years. How hard could working a plane be compared with working bingo night at the Trafford Polish Club?

For years, both my grandmother Ethel and Polish Club regulars like Mrs. Cupka were sure the bingo games were fixed. Someone, that fat Eddie Chesky probably, had tampered with B12, they said. They swore they saw B12 loll around on the bottom of the pile while all the other balls bounced and whirled. Mrs. Dzurka, who was afraid of my two-hundred-plus-pound grandmother, said Mrs. Cupka was full of *drecka* and that B12 came up at least twice a week, but Mrs. Cupka was too senile to remember that.

If I could pry Mrs. Dzurka's good-luck kewpie doll out of Mrs. Cupka's clenched fist all those years ago, I certainly could, now that I was a full-blown adult, handle almost anything the average airplane passenger could dish.

I told myself I'd use the flight-attendant gig as a way to get to New York, where I'd finally begin my life as a real writer. Plus, being a flight attendant would provide great material. I'd get to see the world.

During Season 3, Ann Marie wins a beauty contest and

is dubbed Miss New York Has Everything. During the talent competition, she makes a cheesecake with all New York ingredients. She looks forward to representing the city during appearances in exotic locales like Albany and Buffalo.

During my airline interview at the Pittsburgh Hilton, a woman named Randi, who had huge teeth and a cottonball accent, told me I'd be based in New York and have five-day layovers in Paris. I pictured myself in cafés, reading Baudelaire, drunk on wine—not a 7-Eleven, bingo hall, or big fish in sight.

I said, "Where do I sign?"

I didn't know that there was no such thing as a five-day Paris layover unless the wings fell off the plane. I didn't know that, even though I'd be based in New York, I'd more often be holed up in a Best Western someplace exotic like Albany or Buffalo, checking for bugs in the bathroom and living on saltines and lukewarm room-service soup.

Randi told me she lived in the West Village, off Christopher Street, in a beautiful brownstone. What she didn't say is that she probably had four roommates so that she could afford the rent on her flight attendant's salary. She told me I'd be based in New York.

"The greatest city in the world," she said, glazing over the fact that first I'd have to spend six weeks in Atlanta, Georgia, training in the art of in-flight service.

All of my fears of flying kicked in the day I had to board the plane that would take me to Atlanta. I had 3A, a nice complimentary First Class window seat, with a perfectly nauseating view of western Pennsylvania's patchwork terrain. I thought about all the people I'd left on the ground and for a minute I felt lost. This surprised me. It would always surprise me, the way this feeling would come on for years. But mostly, I felt light, a helium balloon that escaped from some mini-mall grand opening, then lifted up and out of reach.

Randi, a grown woman who dotted her i's with chubby hearts and salted everything she wrote with exclamation points, had told me that, if I made it through training—a big if, since believe it or not many flight attendants flunk out during the first week or two, either because they keep missing their 4 AM wake-up calls or because they can't memorize all the world's airport codes—I'd earn my wings. I'd become a perfect flying machine, able to simultaneously restrain drunks, balance trays of hot coffee over sleeping passengers, and administer either Cokes or oxygen with aplomb.

But first I'd have to make it through this flight.

The engines roared and rattled and the huge tube catapulted down the runway. The plane seemed to be having trouble lifting off, like a fat kid trying to dunk a basketball. When the nose bobbed, then miraculously lifted up, I realized that I hadn't been gripping just my armrest. I had a good and very sweaty hold on the expensive-feeling sleeve of the businessman seated next to me. He was looking at me as if I smelled.

Still, I wanted to make friends. For all I knew, this man

could have been the last person I saw before I died. I made a few jabs—"What's your name?" "Fly much?" Then he whipped out a monogrammed eye mask, pulled it tight over his perfectly coiffed gray hair, and instantly faked sleep, adding a dignified snore here and there for effect.

I had to stop myself from giving in to the weird urge to take just a corner of his sleeve between my thumb and forefinger, to rub it again, this material that was softer than anything I'd ever felt. I don't know why I wanted to do this. Maybe for luck.

This was March 1994. There'd been snow the week before, and the cold front meant that the flight wasn't smooth. I was terrified. I hit my call button so often the flight attendants had to tell me to knock it off.

In Episode 90, "The Snow Must Go On," Ann gets snowed in at JFK. In Episode 98, "Write Is Wrong," Donald writes a script about Ann being snowed in at JFK. He leaves out the messy details—like the fact that Ann's father, Lou, was stockpiling stolen sandwiches in an airport locker, building a makeshift survival kit in case the snow never let up.

Donald focuses on Ann, how beautiful she was, how she conquered her fear of flying, how eager she was for her career and her plane to take off.

Bored by my seatmate, who, no longer faking, was officially asleep and drooling on his own elegant shoulder, I worked up my courage and spent the last half of the flight staring out my window. I tried to distract myself from thinking about how it might feel to fall thirty thousand feet. Instead, I looked for shapes in the clouds, a game I've loved since I was very young. In place of the usual suspects—a cloud poodle, muffin, or elephant—I saw cities, skyscrapers and bridges and roadways, balanced in midair. Somewhere underneath it all were the real cities—Pittsburgh, New York, Atlanta—but there was no telling for sure. I could have been headed anywhere or nowhere. Already the lines were blurring.

where's the glamour?

I'd hoped for something a bit more *That Girl*—pillbox hat, white gloves, maybe even a cute pilot named Donald who'd offer to carry my bags.

Instead, there I was in the cramped galley of a 757 on a flight to Fort Lauderdale, stuffing a meal cart full of gnarled chicken and cold coffee. Coffee was spilling everywhere, soaking through my snappy polyester pants to my skin.

At times like these, when it was nearly impossible for me to smile, passengers always wanted to chat. And so I wasn't surprised when a woman came into the galley and said, "Those seats are made for midgets. My veins are in knots. Give me some water and one of those cookies, would you, doll?"

She wore a red-satin jogging suit and huge fake Armani sunglasses with sculpted gold lions roaring from the temples. She downed the bottle of water in two sips, then paced and waited for the lav to open up. I went back to work, hoping she'd leave me alone, but then she leaned down and poked my spine. I got a whiff of Aqua Net, musk, and corned beef.

She was a close talker, so cookie crumbs and spit were flying when she said, in a perfect Brooklyn accent, "Honey, you girls work so hard, so hard you work. I think to myself, hey, where's the glamour? Tell me, doll, where's the glamour?"

Even before I earned my wings, I knew the movie-style glamour I'd imagined was going to be hard to come by. There were hints during those six weeks of brain-sopping training, where I mastered proper peanut distribution, beverage-nap alignment, and creative ways to restrain passengers with blankets, plastic handcuffs, or simply by sitting on them.

I had a certificate that said I was an expert in Verbal Judo—a passenger-management technique that employs empathy and aggression, as in "Sir, I understand you've had a long day and would like a sixth Scotch; however, I need you to pull up your pants and get off the beverage cart right now."

And then there was Fitting Day.

Fitting Day was supposed to be a rite of passage, marking our transformation from groundhogs to sky goddesses. We didn't know that the companies that made airline uniforms also made getups for janitors.

When the big day came, even Brooke, my completely nondelusional friend, had brought a camera.

"Do you think they'll be able to do something with these?" she said, twirling an imaginary hula hoop with her hips while I eyed my own butt in the three-way mirrors our instructors had brought for the occasion.

Brooke was a former pharmacist's assistant from Ellwood City. She'd been hired with me back in Pittsburgh, and quickly became my perpetual flying buddy and best friend. Brooke has the kind of classic Italian face and long wavy hair Botticelli loved to sculpt. She also has huge blue eyes, which, on her first trip to Rome, would cause two men, both named Paolo, to follow her up and down the Spanish Steps, saying, "Your ice. Your ice remind me Paul Newman." She didn't pay attention to any of it. This, along with her kindness and sense of humor, makes her infinitely lovable.

I suppose Brooke was running away like I was, though she didn't seem to think about or romanticize it much.

"Toss some peanuts, hustle Cokes. How hard could it be?" she said. "If that's what it takes to get to have lunch in Rome, peanuts and Cokes for everybody, on me."

Brooke's story wasn't much different from mine. It included yet another dead western Pennsylvania mill town, a drunk ex-fiancé, a father who was big in the Ellwood Sons of Italy, and the recent loss of her pharmacy job.

The ex-fiancé cheated repeatedly with a skanky woman with bad teeth who could have been Bix's partner in rehab. When Brooke broke up with him, he was distraught. He'd taken to following her around in his Jeep. He'd blow his salary on beer and on Sons of Italy raffle tickets, which he'd buy to get cozy with her dad. He'd resorted to pleading with Brooke's family and friends to convince her to take him back.

As for Brooke's dad, he had started managing Sons of

Italy loans. People started to show up at Brooke's house at night with little sacks of gold jewelry or, once, a pig as collateral.

"Really, it was just a picture of a pig. My sisters and I thought we'd adopted him, like a pet," Brooke said. "You know, the way you can adopt elephants in Africa. Then one night my dad came home with enough bacon and ham for a month. I figured something was up."

As for her former boss, the pharmacist, he'd been jailed for selling amphetamines without prescriptions to fat Ellwood City housewives, and the pharmacy had closed down.

"It's sad, really," Brooke said. "He did a good business."

Brooke had been working part-time as an aerobics instructor, taking in her pharmacist's former clients, when she saw the ad in the *Post-Gazette*. Which is, of course, what brought us together in this room at our airline's training center.

After all those quizzes on airport codes and lessons on how to deal with projectile vomiting, we were eager for the bit of glamour that, we hoped, was finally coming our way.

But then the company fitters arrived, with their cardboard boxes full of plastic-wrapped bundles. They tossed us each a standard-issue dress—"designed to flatter all figures."

The dresses were vertical sacks, with shoulder pads that could double as oven mitts. They were meant to accommodate those senior flight attendants who'd spent years gnawing on Gouda in Business Class and stockpiling French butter pats in their carry-ons.

"Cheer up," one fitter told me. "At least you don't have to wear girdles anymore."

Then she handed me an apron.

Across the room, Brooke was already modeling hers. She plunged her hands into the deep pockets and flipped the apron's skirt up like a cabaret dancer. Later, on flights, she'd strap on her apron and stuff the pockets full of peanuts, cookies, Band-Aids, sugar packets, airsickness bags, tampons, tea bags, napkins—anything she thought she'd need.

"Saves time," she'd say. "Besides, we can't let these designer pockets go to waste."

Inevitably, she'd forget to take off the apron and would parade through the airport concourse like an escaped chef from Burger King, the sound of crinkling cellophane and foil-wrapped peanuts marking her every step.

Like Burger King's, our uniforms, aprons included, were stain-resistant, heavy-gauge polyester and, most likely, flammable. They matched the industrial carpeting that lined the floors and walls of the planes.

This, I began to believe, was no accident.

It's helpful if passengers see flight attendants as parts of the airplanes. That way, we're easy to blame for just about anything. We can deliver straight-faced messages about "rough air" and "deplaning." We can be expected to smile while handling warm airsickness bags and leaky diapers, or while the remainders of strangers' dinners dribble into our shoes.

"It's like we're not even human," I'd tell Brooke.

"Lighten up," she'd say. But some flights, like the Fort Lauderdale one, were tough.

This was not the life I imagined.

After a month or so of whining, I decided that, if I couldn't lighten up, at least I would make the best of it. I had my dress cut to fit. I learned how to do my hair in a French twist and Brooke, an accessorizing expert, taught me how to tie my uniform scarf in a loop called, in illustrated company handouts, "The Noose."

"If things get too bad, you can just pull really hard," she'd say, then bulge her Paul Newman eyes, stick out her tongue, and pretend to choke. "It's like cyanide, but much more fashionable."

Despite the evidence that there was, in fact, very little day-to-day glamour, many of the people I knew dug their acrylic claws into the old-Hollywood version of flight-attendant life and wouldn't let go.

Take Anastasia, for instance.

Anastasia is "former Pan Am."

When Pan Am—that Caesars Palace of airlines—folded, Anastasia and many of her counterparts went off to slum at major and minor U.S. carriers that had as much in common with Greyhound as they did with Pan Am. "Former Pan Am'ers" bitterly remember the days when flight attendants carved prime rib in First Class, wore natural-fiber uniforms designed by Pucci, didn't suffer from hammer toes or carpal tunnel, and actually did have pilots who'd carry their luggage.

A few of those folks, Anastasia included, have even written books about those good old days, girdles and all. Anastasia always carried her book in her roll-aboard, and sold copies to younger flight attendants, saying, "You really must read what your life could have been like."

On the cover of her book, there's Anastasia in her old Pan Am glory. She's standing on a tarmac, jet exhaust blowing so that she has to hold her cap at a jaunty angle with one gloved, pinkie-extended hand. Her hips are thrust out, ready to greet the world. She looks younger, much younger, than the Anastasia I worked with, but her smile has stayed the same. She looks like she's going to bite.

Now, I don't know many details about Anastasia's life, and we all have fantasies we keep in order to go on living. Me, I've got my own catalog. Besides, Brooke had told me recently that Anastasia had started taking antidepressants, and the drugs seemed to be helping, so I should be gentle. The problem was, I was forced, on too many occasions, to work with her.

And she was mean.

She called passengers livestock. She said things like, "Back at Pan Am, these stinking livestock couldn't put together enough change to buy a ticket"; and "These livestock don't need a beverage service. They need a trough."

She believed that everyone smelled. Not just passengers, but everyone.

Throughout a flight, she'd coat her hands with perfume and prop her index finger under her nose like an aromatherapy mustache. And although she claimed it was a safety concern, I suspect it was something more personal that drove her not to sit on her jumpseat for takeoff and landing.

On the jumpseat, she'd be forced shoulder-to-shoulder, thigh-to-thigh, with another flight attendant, and, like I said, she believed everyone smelled. Whenever I flew with her, she preferred to sit in any open passenger seat, saying that, in the event of an emergency, the livestock would be able to open their own pens.

She was, in short, hateful.

So what.

The real problem I had with Anastasia was that she did not work. She believed the job of a modern-day flight attendant—which includes everything from cooking and serving meals to performing the Heimlich maneuver when a passenger chokes on a tendon—was so cavernously beneath her that she refused to do just about anything.

Sure, she'd go through the motions on a beverage cart, one finger creeping up beneath her nose as she handed out Cokes without ice ("Civilized people do not use ice"). She'd even hand out meals, shoving them at passengers like a math teacher doling out F's.

But find a pillow?

Answer call lights?

Perform CPR?

Forget about it.

Anastasia would gather up her bottle of perfume and barricade herself in the bathroom, the galley, or the cockpit whenever possible. She'd become so absorbed in applying extra coats of thick red lipstick, chatting up a pilot, or reading the latest *Entertainment Weekly* that she could block out the very existence of other flight attendants in need.

"You want to be a garbageman?" she said to me on one flight when I asked for help on the trash cart. "You go ahead."

Of course, we all have our fantasies.

Anastasia truly did not see herself as a flight attendant. She certainly did not see herself as working class. When she'd hold court in the lounge, she'd tell rookie flight attendants that she was really an actress. She kept flying only because she'd grown accustomed to buying her groceries in Paris.

And there was some truth there. Back then, groceries were cheaper and better in Paris than they were in New York, and Anastasia was definitely a regular in the extras circuit. She may even have been a member of the actors' union. Her major claim to fame was a recognizable shot of her among the crowd of antiwar protesters in the Washington, DC, scene in *Forrest Gump*. Until a supervisor made her stop, Anastasia was bringing copies of *Forrest Gump* to the LaGuardia lounge and repeatedly playing the one-second clip of her, signature snarl in place, giving a lopsided peace sign.

"Back at Pan Am, we were all actresses or models,"

she'd say. "Now look at the people they let fly. No class.
And hips so wide they can't fit through aisles without taking someone's eye out."

Oddly enough, those hips usually belonged to flight
attendants of Anastasia's generation—people who'd spent
years on international flights, gobbling leftovers and taking home smoked salmon and caviar to feed their cats,
whom they referred to as babies or darlings and dressed up
in Santa hats and beards for Christmas.

I always wanted to let Anastasia know that—while my
own illusions of glamour were nearly sucked dry by my
uniform fitting, my first overnight in Ohio, and the classy
MARRY ME, FLY FREE T-shirts hawked at the company
store—my training class still had its share of model-slash-
actresses. The standouts included two Hooters calendar
girls and one former professional cheerleader. All of them
were, if not purely glamorous, beautiful enough to seem
like a different species.

The cheerleader, Cynthia, was, I suppose, as close as
our class came to producing another Anastasia. Cynthia
was the embodiment of a flight attendant from those Pan
Am days, at least as Anastasia had described them. No
matter what time of the day—predawn, noon, midnight—
Cynthia gleamed. Her white-blond hair, when illuminated
by fluorescent lights, hurt my eyes. Her teeth were mini-
novas, which she relentlessly brushed and flossed. Her
nose was a carved wedge of cheese. Even her nostrils were
in perfect proportion, each exactly the same size, like tiny
kidney beans. Her lips were thin, but popped just a bit in

the middle, as if she were forever sucking on a gumdrop. She wore little flowered sundresses that clung to her pretty fake breasts. Wedged white sandals showed off her meticulously manicured feet, their toenails painted conch-shell pink.

You may have seen her. Since our time together at the training center, she's gone on to become the star of the company's safety videos, brochures, timetables, and baggage tags.

Even in her polyester uniform, even in that ridiculous noose scarf, Cynthia looked amazing, the epitome of high-flying grace.

In short, Cynthia was and probably continues to be perfect. During training, Cynthia was a blond Audrey Hepburn. I was Janeane Garofalo—the bad-tempered version, before she gave up caffeine, took up feng shui, and started working out with a personal trainer.

This was something I had to face every day when, in a flashback to my Junior Miss days, I rolled into my seat, barely on time, my long wavy hair a mess, stray strands on my shoulders and back, a smudge of cream cheese on my cheek, a smear of mascara under my eyes, a new zit breaking through at the tip of my somewhat off-center nose, my nail polish chipping off.

Cynthia, alphabetically assigned to sit next to me for two weeks of training, was, I could tell, horrified. It's not that she'd do anything as obvious as raise a perfumed finger to her nose. But she would lean away, line up her collection of pastel-colored milky pens like a Berlin Wall between us, and become fascinated by her cuticles whenever I entered the room.

Although mostly she tried to avoid eye contact, she couldn't help glancing over once in a while, to take in the disaster. She'd look particularly offended whenever I took out my previous day's notes. One time, as I was unfolding the notes, which did, in her defense, look like the beginnings of a giant spitball, she couldn't keep it in.

"Why are your notes such a mess?" she said, her waxed eyebrows arching into S-curves.

Cynthia kept her notes in a purple folder. Cynthia's notes were highlighted in pink. She had rainbow-colored flashcards and chubby flowery handwriting. She drew big puffy clouds around all her airport codes. She used exclamation points: "ATL is for ATLANTA!"

"Huh?" I said, chugging the last of my morning coffee, trying to wake up before the day's stimulating lecture began.

Today's topic: polite ways to offer a large passenger a seat belt extension.

"Your notes. They look like they've been out in the rain."

"Oh, that," I said, laughing a little, thinking we were finally going to hit it off. "I like to study in the tub. That way I stay awake. Fear of drowning, you know."

"You take a bath here?" she said, leaning even farther away, as if whatever was crawling on me could jump. "In the tub?"

"Well, yes. Don't you?"

"Do you know how many people have used that tub? Don't you know that's how you can get a disease?" she said.

That was pretty much our longest conversation ever.

We had a few other close encounters, like the time we were paired together to demonstrate the Heimlich maneuver and I, being eager, nearly made Cynthia throw up. Or the time we had to wheel each other in the wobbly onboard wheelchairs, and I pushed too fast rounding a bend and flipped Cynthia over.

Let's just say we never became friends. I'd end up at parties or clubs where Cynthia would be holding forth, but none of her glamour ever sprinkled its bleached fairy dust on me.

After we made it to New York, I'd hardly ever see Cynthia, though I'd hear stories. When she was discovered by the company publicist and began starring in all company promotions—particularly the highly coveted role of safety-video host in both Spanish and English—she really used her star power. She would demand to work only in First Class. Then she'd spend the whole flight flirting with or punishing passengers or, like Anastasia, hanging out in the bathroom, flossing her teeth or touching up her makeup.

Once I heard that she and Anastasia, serendipitously assigned to work a Paris flight together, got into it over whose turn it was to do the coffee service. The fight ended with Anastasia rushing teary-eyed to the cockpit, where she happily spent the remainder of the flight.

When she wasn't on layovers, Cynthia took to wearing

huge dark glasses and a head scarf or a designer ball cap. She wouldn't go out alone in New York, not even to walk to the grocery or post office. Men, she said, were always following her. Because of the safety video, she said, people recognized her on the street.

"You don't know what it's like," she told Brooke once. "You just don't know."

"Oh, puhleeeze," I'd say whenever I'd see the latest picture of Cynthia glittering on a company brochure. "I mean, come on now. Who's she kidding?"

I tried to peg Cynthia as a phony, but that wasn't right. Sure, the rumor on the line was that she'd had her boobs and her nose done, but still, she was what she was. I was what I was. If anyone was in denial about that, it would have been me.

Of course I wanted some authentic *That Girl* sparkle in my life. Even more, I wanted my friends and family to buy the idea that I had become a better person, sophisticated, worldly. I don't know why this mattered. It might have been something as simple as not wanting to seem like a failure. I had, after all, run off and joined the circus, as far as most people in my life were concerned. If you're going to join the circus, it's better to be a bareback rider or a trapeze artist than the person who mops up after the elephants.

And so, if I couldn't find glamour in my job, sometimes I'd make it up. On visits home, I'd catch myself doing Cynthia imitations—the fake-Hermès scarves, the Rolex knockoffs I bought on Canal Street for twenty bucks, the sunglasses indoors, the pronounced catwalk swivel, the kiss-hello. I said ciao. I said darling. I'd become, in short, impossible.

"I love the lifestyle," I'd say to my earthbound friends, sighing. "I can go to Paris anytime I want. It's my dream, really. But it's exhausting. You don't know what it's like. You just don't know."

gone native

Not only was I not glamorous. I was also not a German speaker.

This is what I told Sheldon in Scheduling when he called, for the third time in one month, to give me another twenty-four-hour layover in the industrial wasteland of Frankfurt, Germany.

"Sheldon," I said. "Sheldon, I do not speak German. I do not like schnitzel. Riesling makes me break out in a rash, Sheldon, a rash. Passengers do not like a flight attendant with a rash handing them their food. Sheldon, check your computer. Sheldon, there must be some mistake."

"Let's see. Employee number six-zero-seven-nine-six-six-five. Rotation number zero-three-zero-zero-five-zero. That's Frankfurt, all right, sure enough. Come on, now. Y'all just hop that pond and have a beer on me."

Sheldon was funny like that. More often than not, when I got a call from Scheduling, it was Sheldon. I think he was assigned to me, like a Terminator.

I'd never met Sheldon in person, but I knew his voice on the first drawled-out syllable. Sheldon always sounded like he had a tongue depressor in his mouth. Hello, in Sheldon-speak, sounded like damnation. And where my assigned trips and I were concerned, it almost always was.

One of my roommates, Al, whose cousin is the country singer Alan Jackson, a factoid he used to pick up girls who wore little flowery dresses and liked to line dance, always ended up with long layovers in warm places. He recommended that I do the neighborly thing and fly on down to Atlanta to say hey howdy hey to Sheldon in the hope that it would change my luck.

"Just press the flesh a bit, pass him a nice bottle or two," Al said. "Next thing you know, you'll be kicking back, nice and easy, in Nice."

Al, who was also from Atlanta, sounded like he had a tongue depressor in his mouth, too, especially when he pronounced his own name.

I imagined Sheldon looked a lot like Ron Howard, if you crossed Ron Howard back in *Happy Days* with Ronald McDonald. Sheldon, I was sure of it, had a huge red Afro, wore saddle shoes, and smelled like a blend of Wrigley's spearmint, sausage gravy, and Palmolive dish soap.

I had eight roommates, including Al, and we were all under Sheldon's thumb. I probably should explain that having eight or more roommates isn't unusual for airline folks, especially ones based in New York, where rent is insane. Most airline people spend a lot of time flying and little time at their home base, which makes the idea of crash pads—apartments meant more for sleeping than living in—popular.

My roommates and I shared a furnished two-bedroom apartment in Kew Gardens, Queens. When I say "furnished," I mean in the freshman-dorm sort of way. We had wall-to-wall bunk beds and a pullout sleeper sofa. At thirty, I found the adjustment a bit difficult, and would sometimes dream that, if I'd only open a closet door a bit wider, I'd find my very own bedroom, with a full-size bed and a window with a view, inside.

But dreams are dreams, and even when we were pulling straws to see who got which room or who got the top or bottom bunks, I knew things could be worse.

Our landlord specialized in renting to airline employees, who flocked to Kew Gardens because it was close to both LaGuardia and Kennedy airports. He knew all about crash pads, and exactly which kinds of carrots to dangle.

"Here, you each have your own bed," he said, explaining why our rent was twenty-five hundred dollars a month in a neighborhood where the cultural watermark was some drunk pilot singing "Danny Boy" on karaoke night at Yer Man's Irish Pub. "Some places, you're lucky if you get clean sheets."

When I fantasized about New York, I did not count on Queens, with its one stubby skyscraper and its nondescript run-down neighborhoods that reminded me of places I wouldn't want to live in back in Pittsburgh. After a couple of years of flying, I graduated to Manhattan and spent almost nine months sharing a twelve-hundred-a-month studio on the Upper East Side. I believed I'd finally made it after all. Then I found out that my roommate's father

played golf with George H. W. Bush, and that my roommate briefly dated Jerry Springer, had a nose job, a boob
job, and a Rolex. I flew a hundred hours a month and still
had a hard time coming up with my share of apartment
staples, like soap and toilet paper. And so, ultimately, it
was back to Queens for me, where I figured at least I knew
my way around.

My first Queens apartment's most distinguishing fea-
ture was a large permanent roach on the wall in the bathroom. The roach was a good specimen, maybe two inches
long, not counting antennae. It must have gotten stuck
awhile back in a coat of wet paint, and the painters kept
going over it until it was just a bumpy salmon-colored out-
line of a roach, like a mountain in an urban relief map.

The one thing that makes airline apartments and crash
pads livable is the fact that escape is always just a scheduling call away. Sheldon sent Al and the rest of my roommates
to roach-free four-star hotels in gorgeous destinations. Paris,
Lisbon, Madrid, Barcelona, Rome. For me, it was Germany.
Or Cincinnati. I'm not sure which trip I hated more.

Of all the places I'd imagined myself when I first signed
up for this airline gig, Germany wasn't one of them.
Maybe it was World War II. Maybe it was that my friend
Paula, a gorgeous Italian American type, had once spent a
week in Berlin and was almost run out of a grocery
because people thought she was a gypsy. Later, while she
was waiting for a bus, an old man, waddling along with
what looked like a homemade cane, came up and spit on
her shoe.

Maybe it's just that—moral indignation. Or maybe it's that Germany isn't on my list of romantic places. It lacks legendary beaches and literary hot spots. Most German food, strudel and beer aside, makes me sick. And a German opera house or *Biergarten* is, let's face it, no match for the Eiffel Tower, any more than karaoke night at a Queens pub would have been a match for seeing the Ramones at CBGB.

If I were a therapist, I'd say my aversion to Germany also had something to do with my roots. After all, I'm adopted, and although I've never met either my birth mother or birth father, there is that birth name—Amelia Phelan. I know that *Phelan* is Irish—old Irish. I know that it's my mother's name. My father, according to the records my adoptive parents wriggled out of Catholic Charities, was German. He was also married to someone other than my mother. To protect him—or maybe to protect herself (this was, after all, 1964)—my mother refused to put his name on my birth certificate. And so, I've always considered myself more Irish than German, and have always been a bit embarrassed by the übermensch half of my heritage.

Enter Sheldon.

It started during my first month of flying. I think it was a sick plot, but Scheduling seemed to be trying to keep new flight attendants from thinking about our pitiful paychecks, our communal living conditions, and homesickness by shipping us overseas as soon as possible.

My roommates hit the lottery. Me, I got Frankfurt.

"Frankfurt," I said. "Do you have a Paris?"

"It is not appropriate to request a trip," Sheldon said, staccatoing over appropriate and pronouncing trip in two syllables. *Tree-ip.* "Sign in at Kennedy, seventeen hundred hours."

"Thanks," I said.

"Velcum," Sheldon said. He laughed and hung up.

I guess I should have been grateful, and maybe I was a little. Up until this point, my greatest travel adventures had been car trips up and down the U.S. East Coast. I'd reaped the benefits of buy-one/get-one-free coupons at grand Florida attractions like South of the Border and Gatorland—where real Native Americans, wearing baby oil and loincloths, wrestled real alligators the size of lunch counters. And I'd been to Monkey Jungle half a dozen times.

Monkey Jungle—Where the Humans Are Caged and the Monkeys Run Wild.

At Monkey Jungle, human tourists press their oily faces against the glass walls of an enclosed walkway while monkeys pick each other's nits, pee on each other, and otherwise cavort in their "natural" habitat.

Back in the 1970s, Monkey Jungle's main attraction was a vaudeville show held in a small arena at the end of the walkway. The monkeys came out on the hour, suddenly clothed and as civilized as college professors. They wore diapers. They also wore snazzier getups—flowery church dresses, tuxedos, or the classic red shorts and suspenders. They twirled hula hoops and peddled around on scooters and tricycles. Sometimes the chimps danced a polka. Sometimes they were dressed up in headdresses and traditional Native American garb. Sometimes they pretended to live in little tepees, send up smoke signals, or smoke peace pipes.

Had this been a troupe of performing poodles instead of monkeys, my father would have been outraged. And there were and still are many activist groups—especially PETA and Jane Goodall—fighting to close down Monkey Jungle. But when I was a little girl, I thought it was really something. And last I checked, it was still hanging in as one of America's top roadside attractions.

One minute I was a kid throwing monkey chow scooped from a gumball machine at Monkey Jungle, and the next I was deciphering pre-euro German currency on my initial Frankfurt run, courtesy of my good friend Sheldon. There I was, in Germany, my first time, and I never felt more American in my life.

On the flight over, most of our German passengers spoke perfect clipped English and wore funky little eyeglasses. They were, expectedly, overwhelmingly, blond and blue-eyed, and they obeyed orders in a way that only Stepford Wives might. This particular trait distinguished them from American passengers, who refused to do nearly everything and often got in fistfights over seat assignments, overhead storage space, or the last copy of *People* magazine. It distinguished them from the French, who would try to smoke in the lavs, then complain about American puritanism whenever the smoke detectors went off. And it distinguished them from the Russians, who were known to raid beverage carts, take all the vodka minis, and, on at least two occasions at my airline, try to run their fellow passengers over with the carts when flight attendants weren't looking.

On flights to Germany, whenever the seat belt sign was on, there would be a simultaneous click throughout the cabin, like guns loading. When we asked for passengers to bring their seat backs to an upright position, they popped up like toast. They watched the safety demo, following along with the safety information cards they'd pulled from their seat pockets.

It is not right, I know, to generalize about groups of people. But this is how it was on nearly every German flight I worked, and I worked a lot of them. A German passenger's willingness to follow rules is one of the few things that made my frequent routes tolerable.

Although my eyes are green and my cheekbones are high and sharp—mostly Irish features—I am blond, and I have a kind of Eastern European nose, rounded out at the tip. I recognized myself in most of the German passengers, and most of the passengers recognized the German in me, so they were kind at first. They'd speak to me in German, then get annoyed when I could not—or, as many of them believed, would not—answer.

I'd say "*No sprachten die Deutsche*," or under my breath "*sie machen mich unsinnig*"—you're making me insane. This was about the extent of my German.

When they'd get frustrated, they'd say, "*Budweiser, bitte.*" They'd narrow their blue eyes, size me up. They'd say, "*Amerifrau.*"

On my first Hamburg flight, a jolly old German woman with jowls held me captive in the galley, telling me what I think, based on the rhythm and timing of her delivery, were jokes. She had breasts like bumper cars. She kept leaning forward, and her breasts kept pushing me back. Finally, she had me in a corner against the coffeemakers. She laughed and held my arms, leaned in and laughed and held my face and touched her forehead to mine.

Because she was old and seemed nice and I was very new at this, I laughed and nodded and smiled. For all I knew, she could have been telling me she'd murdered her whole family. For all I knew, she could have been calling me sky slut, monkey ass, flying fuckhead. For all I knew, she might have had a bomb. For what it's worth, she seemed to like me, and I liked her. Maybe we were both insane.

An hour before we landed, we ran out of beer. This is not a good thing on any flight, but it's particularly bad when you're headed to or from Germany. It's comparable to running out of red wine on a Paris flight or tea on a London run.

One man was very upset. He rang his call button and waved me over.

He started to complain in German and my eyes glazed over. It had been six hours of this already.

"English?" he said.

I nodded.

"How can there be no beer?" he said. He looked like Freud—round wire eyeglasses, clipped white beard. He had a creepy habit of wetting his lips with his tongue between sentences. I imagined him with a cigar, nodding, taking notes, saying *tell me about your father and no beer.*

"Sorry, sir, but it's true. I checked in First Class myself. Sorry for your inconvenience."

Flight attendants, I learned, apologize a lot.

"My ticket was expensive," he said, then swooped his tongue over his lips, full circle. "The cost of my ticket includes a meal and beverages. I want a beverage. Now. I want a beer. And I know you speak German. You are rude. As for beer, go down and get more," he said.

He looked directly at my chest. He might have been recording the name on my wings to file a complaint, but since he did look like Freud and I was wearing a new water-lined Miracle Bra, who knew.

"Sir, I do not speak German and there's no downstairs. There's no basement in this plane."

"In cargo. With the luggage. Isn't there any in cargo?"

I just looked at him.

"They wouldn't do this on Lufthansa. Lufthansa would never run out of beer." The seat belt light went on and the man pulled his strap tighter. "Lufthansa is civilized. Lufthansa knows how to treat people. Americans are barbarians. American airlines are nothing like Lufthansa."

I would have liked to have said, *Well, why aren't you flying Lufthansa?* or *Historically, barbarians come from your side of the ocean.*

Instead I said sorry, and handed him some extra peanuts, a cute miniature bottle of Maker's Mark, complete with its dribbled red wax seal, and a pair of plastic wings.

It was raining when we landed in Frankfurt. It was also bone cold. This was early May, but the sky was blustery. Two other new flight attendants and I tried to go exploring at lunchtime, tried to keep our enthusiasm up, but the weather was awful.

We stopped into a little restaurant where a huge woman in an apron made from kitchen curtains rumbled the day's menu at us. She looked like she'd stepped out of a Bugs Bunny cartoon, with her fat red cheeks and hands the size of cantaloupes. I wanted to shout *Hasenfeffer*, but she was terrifying and I was sure she wouldn't get the joke and that she would, in fact, bring me rabbit stew, maybe with a fresh rabbit's head, ears and all, still intact and bobbing. I was sure she would have killed the rabbit herself and, upon inspection, I think I saw dried blood under her short, bitten-down nails.

She looked down at me, really looked down, like she was seeing me through the jungle of hair in her nostrils. She said something in German and waited for me to answer. Then she nudged me hard on the shoulder with her order pad.

I blurted what I'd learned on the plane. *Bier, bitte.* I wanted food. Soup, maybe. Some mashed potatoes. She came back with three beers, clutched by their handles in her right hand, and put them down on the table, hard enough so that the beer sloshed out.

"Achh," she said, and stomped off, looking at us as if we were the most savage customers she'd ever had.

The beer was delicious, heavy and cold, but the woman watched us while we drank. She stood behind the bar, her fleshy arms folded across her battleship of a chest. I'm not sure what we did to incite such hate. Probably she was a girl during the war. Probably she still hated Americans. Probably she had good reasons. After a few trips to Germany, I started to realize this wasn't unusual.

Although we would have liked another beer and another, we buckled and went back out into the rain, hungry, tired, miserable. My two friends wanted to waffle around a bit, maybe shop, but I'd had it. I headed back to the hotel, past bars and cafés and shops with postcards featuring kids wearing spiked collars and blue Mohawks—ACHTUNG, BABY—past the random graffiti, an anarchy symbol here, fresh swastika there, a peace sign dripping blood, whole sentences in German I couldn't decipher. On the side of one café, there was a gorgeous mural of flowers and strawberries and a man who looked like and probably was John Lennon.

Back at the hotel, at least there was Gunnar, the concierge. Gunnar was friendly, in a military way. He spoke perfect English.

"You enjoy the city?" he asked as I handed over the umbrella I'd borrowed. "Nice weather here, no? Good to be home, no? Get back to those strong German roots."

I tried to smile, but I was shivering and my hair clung to my cheeks in wormy strands. The umbrella had been useless. A nice German wind had whipped up, pelting rain I was sure was turning to ice.

"Maybe you might try our fitness center," Gunnar said. "Put some fire back in your blood."

Gunnar's eyes were Crayola blue. When he smiled, his huge white teeth reminded me of ceramic bathroom tile. If Brooke had been with me, I would have said to Gunnar, "Your ice remind me Paul Newman." This would have gotten a laugh from us, at least. But there by myself, soaked to the skin, I kept imagining him on one of those postcards, his blond hair spiked into meringue peaks and spritzed blue. I kept imagining him in leather.

"Fitness center, second floor. There's a masseuse. Very handsome. Good hands." Gunnar winked.

Back in my room, I curled up under a down comforter and switched on the TV. A German soap opera was in progress. An equally blond man and woman pushed and shouted at each other. Soap operas are basically the same all over the globe, so I could almost follow the plot. The woman had been in an accident and lost her memory. She didn't know who she was. The man—her lover, brother, husband, or a combination of two of the three—was trying to make her remember.

"Snap out of it," I think he yelled at her in German. Then he shook her by the shoulders.

The TV drama aside, I was still freezing. That's when I saw the little placard on the desk. Conveniently printed in German, French, and English, it read: FITNESS CENTER AND SPA. SECOND LEVEL. MASSEUSE, SAUNA, POOL.

Sure, Gunnar moved as if he were remote-controlled, but maybe he gave good advice. Not about the masseuse, but a sauna. That, I was sure, would bring me around.

I'd thought to pack my new layover bathing suit—a shiny hot pink bikini I'd ordered, along with the Miracle Bra, from Victoria's Secret. It had been on sale, and the top, cut halter-style, actually made me look like I had boobs. It was a bargain.

I put on the bikini, plus sweats and tennis shoes, and set out for the spa. When I pushed through the door on the second floor, there was no one in the locker room. The locker room door was labeled GEMISCHTE. I had no idea what *Gemischte* meant. Then there was another sign. It read: FKK ZONEN. TEXTILEFREI. I figured *FKK Zonen* meant something like "guests-only zone." As for *Textilefrei*, a Latinate root is a Latinate root. Textile-free. What textile-free meant, though, I hadn't a clue.

Off to the right in the locker room, there was another door with a window. Through the window, I could see a man who looked like Schwarzenegger's double working over another, equally buff man. I could hear the man moaning as the masseuse twisted and pounded and pulled. I could hear the sound of flesh slapping flesh and the man's breath being pushed out of him like he was Tupperware.

I stripped down to my bikini, grabbed a towel, and followed the signs as best I could, breaking down the German words as I went. I passed the pool, which was empty, and headed for the *Saunabereich*.

I could hear voices somewhere in the *Saunabereich*,

though I still didn't see anyone. More than voices, I could hear splashing—the sound of a body plunging into a pool—and then screams. Real screams. The water was, I was sure, freezing. I didn't know why people were jumping into it, but they were, one after another. Splash. Scream. Muttered German. Splash. Scream.

The *Saunabereich* was a maze of halls and nooks. Everything was white—the tiled floor, the walls. Even the light seemed pure and white, not cut through with the usual green of American institutional bulbs.

Although the screams seemed to be getting louder, I still couldn't see the pool when I came to the sauna itself, which was set off in the corner of its own hallway. The sauna was the traditional redwood variety. There was a red light on the front and an illuminated sign with the words BITTE WARTEN—AUFGUSS. I translated this to mean "Please Be Warned—Hot." No kidding. I figured the people who placed that sign might just be related to the people who label airplane peanut packs with the warning: CAREFUL. MAY CONTAIN NUTS.

Outside the sauna entrance, there was a large bucket of ice and some shelves that were full of people's personal effects—towels, shower shoes, robes.

I had to tug hard to open the sauna door. When it finally gave, there was a blast of dry heat and a whoosh of steam. I stopped in the doorway for a few minutes until my eyes adjusted to the dark.

Then everything was clear.

Inside the sauna were half a dozen or so completely

naked people. Men and women, none seemingly under the age of fifty. One man, maybe in his sixties, was standing, bent over, his backside up, facing the sauna entrance. The man was pouring water onto the hot rocks, which spit and sizzled. This seemed dangerous.

I must have stood in the doorway for a while because they all looked at me. They seemed annoyed. I wanted to back up, head for the locker room, but it seemed rude. So I pulled the door shut behind me, brushed past the man working the rocks, and sat down next to another man who, I thought, had a body that looked like a wilting Chia Pet.

Inside that sauna, my hot pink bathing suit glowed.

I couldn't decide what to do. Etiquette, I thought, would demand that I lose the suit. But how? There was no way I could just casually slip it off. And there was no way I was walking out of the sauna and walking back in naked.

I tried to force myself to look around. I couldn't remember what the pilots from the flight over had looked like. I usually couldn't recognize them out of uniform any-way, not without drawing imaginary little pilot's hats on their balding heads. To be naked in front of strange middle-aged Germans is one thing. To be naked in front of two middle-aged American pilots I'd have to bring coffee to on the way home was another.

I thought about Gunnar.

Good to be home. Put the fire back in your blood.

Nice joke. He was probably on his way up here, I thought; any minute he'd prance through the door. Worse, he'd press his face to the little window, like a tourist at Monkey Jungle, and say *Look at that one in her little suit.* Then he'd wait for the others to tear me apart.

But Gunnar didn't show, and after I'd stayed what seemed like a respectable time—long enough to break a sweat—I stood, stretched, and headed for the door. The man was ladling water over the coals again, and I had to brush past him on my way out. A light was on, and again those words BITTE WARTEN—AUFGUSS were bright red.

I pulled at the door. It was stuck.

I was suddenly hot, too hot. I thought I would pass out. I could feel the eyes behind me. Someone muttered something in German. Someone else snorted. Outside there was a splash, another scream.

Behind me, a man's voice, deep and low, said, in perfect English, "Push."

Postscript: Notes on the Traditional German Sauna

Thanks to Naked Man, a writer for www.netnude.com, I've since learned the following:

- *FKK Zonen* stands for "Frei Karper Kulture." This means "Clothing-Free Culture."
- A *Textilefrei Zonen* is a mandatory nude area.
- *Gemischte* means "mixed sex." "You may find yourself in a locker room, undressing next to another man, woman, or a full family," Naked Man writes. "A very liberating experience!"

- *Aufguss* is the time an attendant comes into the sauna and ladles water onto the hot stones to generate steam.
- *Bitte Warten—Aufguss* means "Do Not Open the Door—Aufguss in Progress."
- Do not wear a swimsuit into a German sauna. It's considered unsanitary, even barbaric.

haywire

At the hotel pool, Brooke and I drank champagne and piña coladas, twirling those little paper umbrellas like they were the cigarettes we'd both given up.

Brooke, in her new black bikini, said, "You know we're getting paid for this," and took a long drag on the spiral straw stuck into her coconut-shaped cup.

"We're not getting paid much," I said, slurping back. "But still."

It was almost a hundred degrees at three o'clock in the afternoon in Vegas, where we'd lucked into a thirty-two-hour layover. As flight attendants, our layover pay was just enough to cover meals. But today, in the capital of sunshine and luck, we felt rich.

Earlier that morning, I'd won two hundred dollars playing Haywire, and we were determined to drink it up. Haywire was the world's greatest slot machine, packed with more bells and whistles than a strip club. I loved the lights and the sounds, especially the sound of quarters pouring out while a red cop-car light spun wildly, announcing to everyone in the Hard Rock that I was a winner after all.

Brooke, our bar/slush fund aside, wasn't so impressed. She had been lecturing me for hours on the art of gambling, furious that I'd put in only one quarter.

"Look where you'd be now. Two quarters, always two quarters. You have to play the max," she said, peering over the top of her Jackie O sunglasses. "Stop playing it safe already."

What Brooke saw as my tendency to play safe, albeit an odd kind of safe, drove her insane, particularly when she drank.

About a year after we arrived in New York, I met a man named Diego at a dive bar in Queens. I had been seeing him steadily ever since. Brooke hated him. I didn't like him much, either—he was a world-weary cop who scowled even in his sleep—but it was nice to have something to come home to, a check mark on my life's to-do list, and a picture to show and something to say to the nice concerned Jewish ladies on the plane who'd ask, "You have romantic prospects, doll?"

It also didn't hurt to have an almost native New Yorker to show me around. As much as I was in love with New York and its "queer gifts of anonymity and loneliness," as E. B. White once put it, I still needed help decoding subway maps, separating the East Side from the West, and distinguishing between a coffee regular and a light-and-sweet.

Diego, who'd been born in Argentina but lived in Queens since he was fourteen, had a lot of the qualities of the paper-doll New York boyfriend I'd imagined growing up. He was tall, dark, and tough. He had the kind of thick borough accent that made him seem tone-deaf, and he managed to not look ridiculous in a black leather jacket, tight black jeans, and a silver-studded belt.

"He looks like a Spanish Vinnie Barbarino," I'd say whenever Brooke pressed it. "Come on, he's cute. Nice teeth. Good hips. It doesn't mean I've stopped looking or anything."

But the truth was, I had.

When men would give me their business cards on the plane, when they'd ask me out on dates, when they'd chat me up at a bar, I'd nearly always brush them off or stand them up. I stood up a guy for a night at the opera. I stood up another guy for dinner at The Plaza, and another who offered a romantic cruise on the Circle Line. These were nice people offering dream dates, and I simply would not show. I felt horrible about this, and was too embarrassed most days to answer my own phone. I didn't have much of an explanation for my bad behavior, other than I didn't have the time or energy to spend.

My real relationship was with New York. I had pangs whenever my job kept me away from it for long. As E. B. White had promised, New York allowed me to become part of the landscape, just another bright umbrella bobbing in a sea of umbrellas down Lexington Avenue in the rain. On my days off, I'd get up early and take the train into Manhattan where I'd spend the entire day. In the city, I could walk for miles. I'd invent errands for myself. I'd go in search of lettuce or raspberry soap and come back hours later, usually forgetting whatever it was I'd planned to bring home.

I was devoted to all the city's small joys and indulgences—corner groceries where deli men called me honey; chocolate banana crêpes and red wine at Café Tina; the good jukebox at The Lion's Head; the smell of old books at The Strand; chess players with their stop clocks in Washington Square Park; the beautiful trannies—the only people I've ever met other than my friend Trish who really know how to use liquid eyeliner—on Christopher Street.

As far as men went, what I needed was an anchor, and for that, Diego would almost do. The problem was, aside from being cute and somewhat helpful, Diego did not have much in common with *That Girl*'s Donald.

Before he became a cop, a job he loved because it allowed him to draw John Wayne lines between the good guys and the bad guys, he'd been an Army Ranger. He never saw combat, and was sad about this. He had tried out for Special Forces, but didn't make the cut. The latter, he said, was the reason he left.

"I couldn't respect myself after that," he said.

On our first date, he talked nostalgia—swamps he'd slept in, bugs he'd eaten, how he'd survived a flesh-eating foot fungus. Then he made me watch a CNN tape of himself competing in a "Best Ranger" tournament.

"It was the greatest thing I ever did," he said, then rewound the tape, freezing to an image of himself going hand-over-hand on a rope bridge like a demented mud-caked Tarzan.

When they wanted to see the world, people in my family, instead of joining the circus or the airlines, joined the military. When my cousin Cheryl enlisted, she had a smile like Magic Johnson's, a big open laugh, and a gift for making even a knock-knock joke seem hysterical. By the time she got out of the army—and, maybe not so coincidentally, became a cop in Pittsburgh—she'd lost her gift. Instead of laughing out loud during family gatherings, she'd watch TV and provide color commentary to sitcoms.

"That's funny," she'd say without smiling as she'd watch Rachel do a pratfall on *Friends*.

I wasn't a stranger to what the military did to people. There were a lot of cops in my family—five on my mother's side alone—so I knew what being a cop could do, too. And even though I should have known things were going to go wrong the time Diego whipped out a camouflage rain poncho for a walk to the subway, or the time he decided to share a romantic freeze-dried brownie from the military MRE he'd been saving, or the time he insisted that I learn how to clean his Glock, I found reasons to stick it out. Like I said, he was cute.

There was also his grandmother. Shortly after we met, I told Diego I had a graduate degree in poetry. He told me that his grandmother knew Pablo Neruda. She'd met Neruda through her husband, who, back in Argentina, worked for the evil Perón government and, according to Diego, had been assassinated with a poison cigar.

I loved Neruda, his poems of love and despair, his ode to his socks.

Diego's grandmother might as well have known God. I was smitten.

"I have to meet her," I said.

Diego made me wait several weeks, dangling his grandmother like bait. Then he finally relented.

His grandmother was a tough little woman with a tan wrinkled face and pencil-straight posture. She carried herself like the widow of someone who had been important enough to be killed. I knew from Diego that she read palms, visited psychics, and, although she was probably in her eighties (no one in her family knew her real age), she could still do a yoga headstand.

She was terrifying. I was nervous. I had practiced my Spanish, and hoped I could impress her by reciting lines from Neruda, but the words flopped around in my head like beached fish. I did my best, and I'm not sure what I said, but she got the idea.

"So you like the poet, eh?" she said to me in English, her small brown eyes sizing me up.

"Yes," I said. "Very much."

"Ah, Neruda. Let me tell you about Neruda," she said. "Neruda . . ."

And here she paused dramatically.

"Neruda was una Socialista. A Socialist," she said. "And a very messy eater. Food all over his face."

This was all she said.

No matter how often I went to see her, no matter how many questions I had, no matter how long I waited for her to add something, anything new, she always said the same thing.

Still, she had known the man, had been at dinners with him, had been close enough to see the food all over his face.

That, at least, was something.

As for my relationship with her grandson, it was okay at first. All my New York fantasies bopped through my head as we rolled around on Diego's pullout couch, a soundtrack of sirens and car horns seeming romantic in that big-city way. And, like I said, Diego had good hips and, when it came to sex, he used them with a kind of Best-Ranger intensity. But if I thought about it, which I didn't at first, there was something weirdly mechanical going on, as if he were timing himself, keeping track of which parts of my body he'd touched.

He'd say, "You like that, baby?"

He'd say, "Yeah, you like it."

And then there was the circumcision.

A month after we met, Diego got a call from someone at the VA hospital. This was, the voice said, his last chance. Diego, like many Spanish and South-American-born men, had never gone under the knife. The army knew this, and was calling to tell him his rights to this particular free medical benefit were about to expire.

Of course he scheduled an appointment.

"Just want to see how the other half lives," he said.

I dropped him off and picked him up at the hospital. He was loaded up on painkillers and heavily bandaged, a mummy wrap job. As it turns out, the doctor who worked on him was a med student, and, ancient bandaging techniques aside, probably not a very good one, judging from the scars he'd leave behind. The army was, it seems, calling in its uncircumcised troops to give its future field surgeons practice. Apparently, if soldiers are at war and have to be "in the field" for a long time, circumcision becomes a hygienic necessity.

"Think toe jam," Diego said. "But worse."

Diego was out of the army. He wasn't going to the field anytime soon. Blood seeped through the bandages.

"That looks painful," I said.

"You have no idea," he said.

What I had no idea about was what kind of thirty-something man would be willing to get circumcised just to see what it would be like.

Pain, Diego said, builds character.

"Sure, I said. "But that's life pain, heartache, that sort of thing. It doesn't mean you have to put your body parts into a food processor."

I began to think Diego was not quite right.

"You need to get out more," Brooke would say. And then she'd try to fix me up with pilots or vitamin salesmen from Business Class.

I should have followed Brooke's advice because I could have used the free vitamins and things with Diego just kept getting worse. When he found out I was a writer, he did more than just lure me with his Neruda connections. He started a journal. He used one of those diaries I had as a teenager, with the tiny lock-and-key on the cover. The diary was stored in the right-hand drawer of his desk, and

he always made a point of putting it back in the same position each time. I'd find out later that he'd booby-trap the
drawer with pieces of dental floss or thread just to see if
anyone, meaning me, had bothered to snoop.

This was one of those useful life skills he'd learned in
Ranger school.

"Curiouser and curiouser," he'd say, cryptically quot-
ing *Alice's Adventures in Wonderland* whenever he spotted
a thread out of place.

I still don't know why, but I stayed with him for years.
My friend Judy says you don't ever have to explain anything when it comes to whom you do or do not sleep with.

"Matters of the heart," she says. "Don't analyze. Just
report."

Usually, right when I'd decide I'd had enough and was
ready to dump Diego, I'd be off on another trip. Alone in
a hotel room, I'd forget and would dial his number, happy
to have someone to call, happy to imagine being missed.
When I got back to New York, he'd be there at the airport
to pick me up, sprawled out on the hood of the pieced-
together car he'd most likely snagged from a chopshop in
Flushing. I'd be miserable. Three days later, I'd be off on
another trip, and things would go on from there.

"It's getting old," Brooke would say, and I knew she
was right.

"You're a good friend," I'd say.

"I'm going to kill you," she'd say. "They'll never find
the body."

In the Diego wars, Brooke had some victories. She'd

encouraged me repeatedly to hook up with a sweet Irish accountant from the Bronx who was, like Brooke, a rabid Yankees fan. And she'd introduced me to a handsome blond detective from Scotland Yard during a two-day lay-over in Manchester.

"He's beautiful," she said, pulling me aside in the woody pub she and I had stumbled on hours earlier. "Don't blow it."

The detective seemed sweet and harmless. Growing up, I'd read many Agatha Christie novels, so a man from Scotland Yard had a certain appeal. And even though I know that being a detective with Scotland Yard is not the same as being a member of Her Majesty's Secret Service, I couldn't help but feel I'd been plopped into a James Bond movie, one where the script called for a small-town American girl to seduce a dashing Brit detective by asking him to explain the phrase *cheeky monkey*. It didn't hurt that, according to the detective, I looked exactly like his first love. And it didn't hurt on my end that he looked like Willie Aames, the 1970s teen heartthrob whose *Tiger Beat* centerfolds mingled with Shaun Cassidy's on my bedroom walls back in the days before Willie bloated up, lost most of his hair, and took to wearing bandannas.

When the detective said, "What's a gorgeous girl like you doing in a place like this?" his royal accent made the cliché seem serious and sincere, and I ended up spending the night with him in my room at the Palace Hotel. We drank wine one of the pilots had pilfered from the plane. We lounged around in plush hotel robes. The rooms at the

Palace were perfect for a bodice-ripping romance—cathedral ceilings, a fireplace, heavy red-velvet drapes, a woodframed bed suited for Henry VIII. In the morning, we ordered room service—one of everything on the complimentary menu, including kippers—and he threatened to have my flight canceled so that I'd have to stay in Manchester for one more day.

"I could say it's a security concern," he said, and then gently wrestled me back onto the bed.

I never saw him again. He'd given me his phone number, and I called once, but hung up when a woman answered. I'd given him a fake number, maybe because of Diego, maybe because I knew from the start that it was what it was. Despite a flight-attendant stereotype, the night with the detective was my only one-night stand, and I don't regret it. There, with this stranger I fuzzily remember as a sweet man who, having just lost his father, liked to talk as much as he liked sex, I began to invent a new life for myself, one that didn't need an anchor, a Donald, a Diego. I felt the same way I felt whenever the plane took off. I never wanted to leave New York, but I had a feeling of release and possibility when the wheels left the runway. No matter where the plane was headed, I always felt, in that moment—one of the most dangerous when it comes to flying—that whatever was on the ground stayed there. I was free, filled with the delicious feeling that I could disappear.

This is the same feeling I carried with me on my layover in Vegas. It's why, along with the cold drinks and my two-hundred-dollar jackpot, I was so happy lounging at that pool with Brooke. Away from the gravity of everything back home, Brooke and I didn't talk about the next day's 5 AM wake-up call, the full flight of cranky and broke passengers we'd have to nurse back to New York, our impending hangovers, Brooke's hammer toes, my lousy back, or our rotten roach-riddled apartment. In our old-Hollywood sunglasses and fresh pedicures, we felt ready for our close-ups. We called the waiter who brought our drinks *darling*. We called everyone *darling*. We laughed loud and scared small children and senior citizens. We draped *People* magazines over our faces to block out the desert sun. This week's exposé: "Brad Pitt's Secret Struggle with Acne!"

"It's not true," I said to Brooke.

"What?" she said, and rolled over onto her belly.

"Brad Pitt," I said. "He may look a little splotchy, but he's beautiful. I've seen him on McDougal Street, picking up after Gwyneth's dog. Designer pooper-scooper."

"Now, that's the life," Brooke said.

"Now that's love," I said. "This, darling, is the life."

the pigeons in
father demo square

When I think about the time I wasted doodling around cafés and wallowing in the misery that was my love life, I remember that day at Caffe Reggio when I sat drinking lattes with my friend Ghislain, watching a group of German tourists try to refold a Big Apple Tours map.

"Big city, big map. It's good to know where you are going," Ghislain said as he ran a finger around the rim of his cup and scooped up a dollop of foam. He held the foam up to the afternoon light and inspected it.

I was used to Ghislain having moments like this. He was from France, after all, and was prone to philosophical introspection. He was also a glassblower. He specialized in large glassblown sculptures of rainbow-infused penises and was in New York to visit galleries, show slides of his work, and hopefully get a show.

When he worked, he liked to drop acid and listen to techno music—two things that seemed odd and out of place in the Old World craftsman tradition of glassblowing. This could also explain his fascination with things like milk foam and bubble bath.

I'd met Ghislain on a flight, Salt Lake City to New York. It had been 5 AM and I was stuck ticketing—not a job I enjoyed, especially on morning flights. Usually, I'd hole up in the galley during boarding. But some days, I'd get stuck and have to whip out survival techniques. I could look right at passengers, say "Welcome aboard," give them their seat numbers, count carry-ons, size up flight risks (Terrorist? Drunk? Psychotic?), and record the color of people's socks, all without making intimate contact.

The morning I met Ghislain, I had a good assembly-line rhythm down. Then I heard this creamy voice say, "Your teeth. You have a little pink smudge."

The voice pronounced it *smooge*.

I looked up to see a man with waves of brown hair, a leather choker, and a pair of Birkenstock sandals—usually disgusting, but in this case they showed off nice feet—pointing at his own toothpaste-ad smile.

"Oh," I said. "Oops. Lipstick." And ran my tongue over my teeth in an unerotic, windshield-wiper move I'd used since puberty.

You might say that, the way my life was turning out, I'd given up on many things, romance among them, but when I got back on the plane, I headed straight to Coach, swapped positions with another flight attendant, and made the lovely Frenchman in 36D my personal quest.

I'd hoped to flirt during the safety demo. There's nothing as irresistible as a grown woman holding a fake oxy-

gen mask to her nose, demonstrating how to breathe normally if the plane goes down. But Ghislain—I'd checked
his ticket stub and knew his name, but didn't know how to
pronounce it (it's *Gee-lawn*)—was asleep. He slept
through the beverage service, too.

"Check out thirty-six-D," I said to my friend Jamie,
who was working the other side of the cart. "He's perfect."

"Oh, honey," Jamie said. "And he doesn't even snore
or drool. You want me to wake him for you?"

I loved to fly with Jamie. Even on awful flights, he
could cheer me up. He had a repertoire of stunts. He could
do a great Lobster Man skit using a pair of oven mitts and
a hotel shower cap. If there was dry ice on board, Jamie
would scoop up a pack and tuck it into his pants, then
strut around the galley saying, "Whew, it's hot in here. Or
is it just me?" When he worked the beverage cart, he liked
to invent conversations that would scare passengers.

On the Salt Lake flight, he'd been telling loud stories
about his fictional parole officer and the cops who were
never going to pin that Reno business on him.

"No, thanks," I told Jamie, and gestured Ghislain's
way. "I just like to watch."

So I was surprised when, later in the flight, while I was
deep into *Glamour* magazine's "100 Steps to a Better
You," I heard that voice again.

"I see we are more awake now," he said. "May I have
juice?"

And that pretty much cinched it.

Ghislain and I spent the rest of the flight talking, while

Jamie, an undercover romantic, did my work for me and occasionally slipped me a hip bump of encouragement. By the end of our chat, I'd learned that Ghislain could recite Baudelaire in both French and English, was influenced as a sculptor by Brancusi (whose sculptures also look suspiciously like penises), and had been in Montreal studying with a world-renowned master glassblower. I'd told him I was a writer, that I loved Baudelaire but could not recite him in any language, and that flying for me was a temporary thing until my life really took off.

Ghislain planned to be in New York for two weeks. Then he would go back to Paris. He was going to stay at the YMCA. Of course, I invited him home.

"My roommates and I, we have a crash pad, we're hardly ever there, lots of bunk beds, better than the Y," I heard myself saying, already certain that my roommates were going to kill me and that Diego would cut up the body.

Ghislain said yes.

When people say nothing happened, they mean sex. And so, between Ghislain and me nothing happened. I explained Diego, about whom Ghislain just shrugged. I became an expert at hiding Ghislain and all traces of him and his glass penises whenever Diego would stop by.

"Affairs are what keep marriages together," Ghislain told me as we sat on a bench in Father Demo Square. He was taking a break from chasing the fat, distracted pigeons who were gorging on pizza crust. On this day, instead of bubbles and foam, Ghislain was obsessed with pigeons.

"They are so beautiful, all those purple feathers. I just need to hold one," he said, and I was sure he was stoned.

"You should have an affair," he said.

"I am not married," I said.

"So no problem," he said. Then he lifted up my hair and kissed my neck. "You will come to Paris. New York is nice, yes, but I will show you the most beautiful city in the world. You will be a writer in Paris. Don't all Americans want this?"

Ghislain had the French gifts of confidence and candor, especially when he was stoned. He could be down-to-earth and pretentious all at once. He also loved to generalize about Americans, the way Americans like me loved to generalize about the French.

I would explain the intricacies of American phrases like *belly button* and *rush hour*, and Ghislain would explain that everything Americans thought was French— French manicures, French vanilla coffee, French poodles, French laundries, french fries—was not French.

"You do not understand the authentic," he'd say. "Everything here is MTV."

Despite his tendency to be weird and direct, my roommates and friends were tolerant of Ghislain. He was, above everything else, charming. And besides, Ghislain could cook. Using a flurry of spices, he could make anything— ground beef, chicken legs, even canned ham—delicious. At a time when my roommates and I were all surviving like pigeons on greasy New York slices and stale pretzels, this was a seductive talent.

During those two weeks, I swapped trips and got time off. I went with Ghislain to visit galleries in SoHo. We talked to curators and showed Ghislain's slides. We checked out glass sculptures of fairies and roses, the kind of kitschy things people in my family would buy from Lenox and display as high art in their china cabinets. Despite the look of the pieces, these were not mass-made by Lenox. They were priced at fifteen thousand and up, Ghislain said, because of the precision of the work.

"To sculpt the vein of a leaf or a feather," he said. "It takes years of study and practice. Very difficult. Like writing, no? Why don't you write more? Because it is difficult? Because you are distracted. You don't have time to focus on the leaf."

"But you don't do leaves," I said. "You do penises."

"But I try," he said. "Someday, I will do a glass penis with wings. That will be new."

Whenever Ghislain talked about his sculptures, I don't think he knew how silly he could sound. I started to wonder if something had been lost in translation, if he meant maybe "cocoon" instead of "penis." Maybe all along he'd been sculpting ballpoint pens. The sculptures were not anatomically correct, so I couldn't be sure. Certainly he didn't get the full gist of what it meant when he said, in his weirdly lyrical version of English, "I love to blow the penis."

Then again, who knows? I probably sounded silly to him, too, prattling on about all the words I wasn't writing. And I probably seemed even sillier when I'd show him the

notes I'd been taking—bits and fragments on cocktail napkins, on hotel stationery—since we met. It was the first
writing I'd done in a while, and I was happy. I attributed
my happiness to Ghislain and our friendship and that particular kind of sexual tension that comes when you're sure
that, no matter what, you're not going to ruin it by sleeping with each other.

"Curiouser and curiouser," Diego said when faced
with my good moods.

Back at the Caffe Reggio, Ghislain told me about the
modeling talent scouts who'd come up to him in
Washington Square Park. They were looking for models for
a new Levi's campaign, and they thought he'd be perfect.
He had only a few days left in New York. They'd given him
their business cards and asked him to call for an audition.

"What did you say?" I said.

"I said I would not be interested," he said.

"Are you crazy?" I said.

I tried to talk to him about money, about the chance to
stay in New York while he waited for a call from a gallery.

"You'll be on a billboard in Times Square," I said.

"Look," he said, and he looked at me the same way, a
few moments before, he'd been looking at the foam from
his coffee. "Do you like the airlines?"

"It pays the bills," I said. "Well, almost. Besides, it's a
way to get to Paris."

"Americans," he said. "Very practical. As for the modeling, I would not be the best. My grandfather, he was a
model. A beautiful man. It was his destiny. Me, I am best

at glass. I cannot waste time doing what I do not love. This modeling I leave to other people."

For years, Ghislain would call me from Paris or Bordeaux. He'd gotten a few shows back home and sold some pieces. Critics said his work was sensual.

"One said I was like Brancusi, if Brancusi knew glass," he said proudly.

He'd set up a small gallery of his own. He worked whenever he wanted to, which was almost always.

"We close when it rains," he said. "Who would come in the rain?"

He said he was happy. He sounded happy.

Those calls always ended the same way.

"You should come to Paris," he'd say.

"Yes," I'd say, and do nothing about it.

Once he called from Montreal, from the studio of the master glassblower.

"I've come back to learn about leaves," he said. "The Canadians, they are all about these leaves. Wings, too. I am so close now. Same continent. How is your writing going? You should come and show me."

I'm not sure, even now, what it was I felt for Ghislain. He was quirky, sometimes annoying. But he was beautiful and honest. Mostly, I think he offered possibility, change. I let him stand in for my illusions, that at any minute my life was going to be everything I'd imagined.

I went so far as to make plans to go to Montreal. I had four days off. I mapped out my flights and worked on a story to tell Diego. I lined up an alibi. I packed.

"I will pick you up at the airport," Ghislain said. "There's a café here you will love."

Who knows anything about the heart?

I never went.

I told Ghislain I'd been called to work at the last minute.

"Yes. Your work," he said. "Well, then. Someday."

"Someday," I said, and in that moment I meant it.

rough air

On postcards, I raved about my layovers.

I scribbled "Guinness is good for you!" on a scratch-n-sniff beer card from Dublin and sent it to my friend Gaina, who still lived in Pittsburgh and had inherited both my leather jacket and my weakness for musicians with nice hair.

On a picture of two girls with blue Mohawks, their nose rings dangling above the word GERMANY, I wrote "My next makeover!" and sent it to Trish.

"The Mona Lisa is tiny and bulletproofed!" I scratched on a postcard from the Louvre and sent it to my parents.

No matter where I went, other than Cleveland, I sent postcards, wanting to keep up my worldly front for all the folks back home. I never mentioned my job itself, because the work was, usually, awful.

This was obvious on rotations like this one, 6 AM, first flight of the day out of LaGuardia.

"New Yawk City to Hot-Lanta," the gate agent in his red coat drawled over the PA. His voice, all syrup and grits, echoed down the jetway to where I was standing, sneaking drags off the coffee I had stashed behind the galley wall.

The red coat's name was Gary. He worked a lot of my flights. Even though my name was on his departure reports, not to mention my wings, he never used it. He called me Darling. He called me Sugar. Sometimes he said, "Hey mama."

I hated him.

Okay, maybe underneath the polyester coat and the dyed biker-black comb-over, Gary was a nice guy, maybe even a fun guy, but I couldn't stand his jokes ("What's the most important part of a head flight attendant's uniform? The knee pads!"). I also hated his willingness to load up an airplane full of drunks, then tell me to have a nice flight.

Maybe it was his accent. Gary was a native of Hotlanta—"Where the sun is hot and the girls are hotter"—and his drawl was gratingly out of place in New York, particularly at six in the morning, particularly when I hadn't finished my coffee.

This morning, before he started boarding, Gary stuck his head in the door and yelled, "How y'all doin'? Ready or not, here they come."

Gary loved to push a flight. All gate agents do. They'd use electric prods on both passengers and flight attendants if they thought it would help set on-time records and earn them the company's coveted Feather in Your Cap award.

The Feather in Your Cap award was, literally, a feather glued to a piece of paper. No raise. No night on the town. No mention in the company's on-board magazine. Just this feather—which looked suspiciously like the ones Ghislain plucked from pigeons—and the words GOOD JOB! HERE'S A FEATHER IN YOUR CAP.

My friend Tammy earned her feather for the time she was racing to catch a flight home on her day off and found this guy unconscious in the food court. She did what she was trained to do—CPR, sans safety mask, sans gloves—until paramedics showed up. Then she ran to her flight, which was already boarding.

She was stopped at the door by a gate agent who said, loud enough for regular passengers to hear, "You're a mess. I can't let you on board looking like that. Go change your shirt and brush your hair and I'll think about it."

Flight benefits, the company tells us, are a privilege. Flight benefits are not a right. There are rules, regulations, dress codes. Flight benefits, the company tells us, can be revoked.

Back when this happened, Tammy was making, as we all were, about ten grand a year. We lived in New York. Our company sent out memos warning us not to show up at the welfare office in uniform. We lived for our flight benefits. Tammy hadn't been home to Norfolk in two weeks.

The gate agent let her on the flight at the last minute and told her she was lucky. A few weeks later, a supervisor in Hotlanta sent the feather, which Tammy stuck on her refrigerator.

As for the man, he lived. Turns out, he was a pajama

salesman and two months later, Tammy got a huge box in the mail. Assorted pajamas, flannel, cotton, imitation silk. The man sent a note, talking about his wife and children, his business, how he didn't remember what happened, how he was happy to be alive, how he didn't even know Tammy's name and had to get it from the paramedics. He hoped that was okay. He wanted to say thanks.

"Pajamas beat a feather any day," Tammy said, modeling a pair of drawstring bottoms covered in red and black Scotty dogs.

So this morning, when Gary said "Ready or not, here they come," I said, "Not," and waved him off.

I was in a mood.

I was nearly always in a mood on early-morning flights, when most passengers came on board exhausted and pissed off, demanding Asiago cheese omelets and cappuccino when they knew they'd get a cookie and crappy airplane coffee with powdered creamer, if they were lucky.

I'd say, "Good morning. Welcome aboard."

They'd say, "I'll have the omelet." Or, on later flights, "I'll have the lobster."

I'd smile and say, "Good one" or "That sounds perfect." I'd smile again, a big landslide that smothered what I would have liked to say.

I had to watch myself. There were so many things I would have liked to say—things beyond commentary on airplane food. But there were those pesky rules, regulations. Just as passengers must never say *bomb* when passing through security, flight attendants are forbidden to give details or use words like *crash,* anything that might incite fear in our on-board guests.

When passengers gave me a hard time about putting their tray tables up for takeoff and landing, I was tempted to explain that, in the event of "impact," tray tables work like guillotines, neatly slicing whatever's behind them in two.

During cabin safety announcements, flight attendants never say, "If there's an explosion." We say, "In the unlikely event of a decompression." We say, "Breathe normally." We do not use words like *storm, tornado, hurricane.* We say, "We're experiencing weather." And we don't ever say *turbulence.* People are afraid of turbulence. We call it "rough air."

By five forty, Gary sent them down, five minutes early, as usual, which left me yawning through my "Welcome aboards," sucking on an Altoid, hoping my lipstick hadn't once again bled onto my teeth. I was having my usual out-of-body experience. I'd just heard my voice say "An omelet? That sounds perfect," when I saw a tiny black woman halfway up the jetway, wrestling with a shoulder bag.

The woman looked about seventy. She was dainty in a Southern, little-girl way, lace and flowers on her dress, her hair in perfect hairdo ringlets. The bag kept throwing her off balance as she bumped toward the plane, into other passengers who harrumphed or said "excuse *me*" or just looked generically mean.

When I say the woman was tiny, I mean the floppy silk

flower on the brim of her hat hit below my shoulder. I bent down and asked if she needed help.

"I don't want to be any trouble, honey," she said. "Don't want a fuss now."

I lifted the bag and slung it over my shoulder, even though I'd been trained not to do this. "Lift passengers' bags at your own risk," the training manual said.

Airlines are always trying to save money by cutting down on the number of flight-attendant on-the-job injuries, and so nearly everything passengers expected us to do—maneuver a beverage cart in rough air, slice lemons, perform the Heimlich maneuver when someone chokes on a peanut during takeoff, restrain drunks when they want to jettison the emergency exits—was at our own risk.

Once, shortly after I started flying, I was working a New York to LA flight. There was a storm. Our L-1011— a dinosaur double-aisle bus of a plane—was hit by lightning. There had been little warning—no calls from the cockpit for flight attendants to be seated, just some bumps and dips, the usual rough air. And so we were picking up trash after a beverage service when there was a flash, then a loud bang. The plane dropped, like an elevator might if someone cut the cable, and I ended up on the floor six rows from where I'd been standing.

I strapped myself into the nearest passenger seat, and had to climb over a man to do it. He'd seen what happened, I'm sure. Still, he was annoyed.

"Don't you have your own seats in the back of the plane?" he said.

I was shaken up, but I wasn't hurt.

Another flight attendant in the plane's lower galley, though, was a wreck. She'd been pinned by a loose beverage cart. Beverage carts, when they're full, weigh more than two hundred pounds.

By the time I made it down to the galley, she was lying on the floor. Another flight attendant was trying to hold her head still. He was trying to calm her down. I'd never seen anyone convulse, and it was terrifying. The woman's arms and legs were in spasms, and she was making a strange sound—it was high-pitched, deep in her throat, not a wail, not a whimper, not like anything I'd ever heard. When we landed, paramedics met the flight and took her off through the cabin service door on a stretcher. When they moved her, she screamed.

Shortly afterward, a supervisor came on board to interview the rest of us. Was the seat belt sign on? Did we think it was safe to be up? Shouldn't all the carts have been locked down?

The supervisor, we knew, was building an argument for the company. The flight attendant should have been seated. The carts should have been in place. She was irresponsible. She had been working at her own risk.

Back on the Hotlanta flight, the little old woman's bag felt like it was loaded with bowling balls. I didn't know how she'd managed it this far, and I told her so.

"Oh, I try and manage what I can," she said. "A girl needs a lot of makeup at my age." She winked, then added, "Don't want to be no trouble, really now."

Just a week before, a woman named Marge was strug-
gling to stuff a bag like this one into a tightly packed overhead
and nearly knocked out another passenger who happened to
be sitting underneath. He was nailed with the corner of what
turned out to be a bag filled with frozen meatballs, two roasts,
and half a ham. I had to fill out paperwork that said just that,
in triplicate. The passenger was fine, but he was demanding a
free round-trip ticket.

As for Marge's bag, it took two of us, plus Marge, to
stow it. While we jammed the bag under an empty seat in
the back of the plane, Marge told us she was headed to
Fort Lauderdale, to visit her daughter.

"My daughter," Marge said, giving the bag one final
shove with her foot. "She likes my cooking."

Did I say this was March?

That meant New York, my beloved island, was a slag
pile, all muck and slush. How nice it would be for someone to show up in March dragging a bag full of meatballs.
How nice it would be to wake up with the sun in Fort
Lauderdale, where, in my limited layover experience, even
the diviest restrooms in the diviest bars smelled like strawberry lip gloss.

On all those drives down the coast, and then with that
pink house in Cape Coral, my father had taught me years
ago that Florida was the Northern working-class dream. It
was the reason people worked like ants for two weeks'
vacation a year. It was where nearly everyone I knew wanted to go to die.

Sometimes I thought I'd be happier if I gave up on New

York and transferred. I told this to Marlena, a flight attendant I met on a turnaround. She herself had transferred from New York to Orlando and seemed to be doing fine.

"Traded sewer gators and Times Square Goofy for the real thing," she joked. "Yuk, yuk."

Marlena was pretty in that typical flight-attendant way. She was older, maybe forty, with chin-length bobbed blond hair and blue eyes. The company likes this look and encourages it. They send hairdressers and makeover artists to the training center and to bases, where they subliminally work to convince most of us that blond and bobbed is the way to go.

Although I fought it at first, I'd started hitting the peroxide. By the time I met Marlena, my hair was nearly white-blond, although it was still too long by company standards and had to be pulled back in a ponytail.

"You have such petite features," one company hairdresser, Phil, told me. "A nice bob would really take the years off. It would make your cheekbones pop."

Phil himself was blond, with yellow highlights. His hair stood up in gelled spikes. He looked like an albino porcupine.

Marlena had high cheekbones, and her hair was cut beautifully. It swept down in a perfect arch and made a J-curve around her jawline. I was sure Phil had nothing to do with it.

On the jumpseat, waiting for takeoff, Marlena and I were chatting. Flight attendants have a ritual called jumpseat therapy. We meet each other, prep the flight, then plop down on the jumpseat and tell the story of our lives in precisely the amount of time it takes for the plane to get off or on the ground. Sometimes, in places like New York, Dallas, or Atlanta, especially, this could be anywhere from twenty minutes to an hour or more.

I don't know why we do this, but we all do. Maybe it's the design of a jumpseat. We're pushed together, our thighs and hips and shoulders touch, and this physical intimacy translates to other kinds of intimacy. Or maybe there's comfort in knowing that, outside any given flight or rotation, we remain strangers and aren't likely to run into each other again soon. Or maybe it's just the nature of the business, the lack of connections on the ground, the transience. Maybe it's the same impulse that leads drunks or vagrants or people on a bus to tell each other their dreams.

Whatever it is, there are flight attendants all over the company who know about my failed dreams, my embarrassingly awful love life. And I know intimate details about people whose names, even now, I can't remember.

But I remember Marlena.

We were on the jumpseat, and I was asking her what brand of blond she was—store or salon, Garnier or Clairol. I wanted to know where she got her hair done, and told her how much I needed a change.

She smiled in an odd way and said, "I go to Bumble. I spend a fortune keeping this thing up. It has to be exactly right, you see."

And then she pushed back the hair from her forehead and right cheek to show me the scar.

The scar was jagged and brownish purple. It looked like drawings I'd seen of arteries, if an artery were ripped open. The edges were serrated, and the skin around the scar toward her hairline was lumpy and looked bruised. Marlena held her hair back and let me examine her face for what felt like a long time. I wanted to look away. Anywhere else, looking away would have been the right thing to do. But on a plane, on a jumpseat, things were different.

"It's been a year," she said.

She'd been living on the Upper East Side, a good neighborhood, expensive, safe, no rats or roaches. She lived in a nice building, a brownstone, four stories, no doorman. She was coming home from a Vegas all-nighter. It was around five in the morning and she was exhausted. She didn't see the man, didn't know where he came from, until he pushed his way through the security door as she was dragging her bag behind her. He started hitting. He beat her so badly the police asked if she knew him because they didn't usually see this much violence in rapes by strangers. He had a razor and he cut her face and arms. He told her he was going to cut her face off. He would have killed her, probably, if she hadn't started screaming and kept on screaming.

"The police said when they came, I was still screaming 'fire fire,' just like they teach you. But I don't remember."

The police caught the guy, she said. There was a trial, a conviction. She had operations.

"I just came back on the line last month," she said. "The company flew me down to Atlanta to meet with a group of supervisors before they'd let me come back. They said it was to see how I was doing. They really just wanted to see how I looked. Can't go scaring the customers now, can we?"

She let her hair fall back perfectly into place and smiled.

The great writer Raymond Carver once said he was a cigarette with a writer attached. Brendan Behan, the Irish playwright and poet, called himself a drunk with a writing problem.

Me, I was a pair of wings with a notebook I never talked about.

I would have liked to have told Marlena this. I would have liked to have told her that I knew, even then, that someday I'd write her story down. I would have liked to have told her why. I would have liked to have said something to her other than "I'm sorry," other than "Jesus Christ."

I would have liked to have said something comforting, whether Marlena needed it or not.

"Last call for Hotlanta." Gary's voice echoed down the jetway, annoying as feedback.

After I took the small woman's bag, she headed for 3B. First Class. I followed her back and managed to lift the bag into the overhead. I handed her the standard mite-infested blanket and pillow, making a show of fluffing the latter until it was almost three-dimensional.

"You airplane people are so sweet. Thank you," she

said, and put one doll-hand in mine. And it was strange, not because she touched me, but because she insisted on making eye contact before she let go.

She was cute and nice. Too nice, it seemed, to be traveling in First Class.

Many flight attendants, like Cynthia, our company spokesperson, choose to work First Class because they believe it adds a certain status to the job. They also believe that First Class passengers are more civilized than Coach passengers. It's not true, of course. This is just something working-class people often think about people with money.

Take the businessman from Westchester County, a very expensive suburb of New York. He was traveling full-fare in Business Class on another airline. He became very drunk midflight, and so a flight attendant cut him off. He was so angry that he went into the galley, climbed on top of a beverage cart, and defecated.

When this story hit the media, no airline person I met questioned whether or not the story was true. The only question was, if the man was so drunk, how did he get on the cart, not to mention balance up there with his pants down, in the first place?

In this kind of world, this nice woman was distinctly out of place.

She didn't ask for an omelet or lobster. She didn't want a fuss. She was polite, even grateful. And on top of all that, because my parents were old and awkward travelers, I'm soft for older people.

Still, I was annoyed.

The bag was ridiculously heavy. My back already ached and I had a twelve-hour day ahead. Even after years of flying, I still wondered why people are willing to lug bags like this one onto the plane instead of checking them. Paranoia, I guess. Employees like Gary don't help, either.

One of Gary's stupid jokes involved a clever acronym for our airline—Don't Expect Your Luggage To Arrive. He liked to tell passengers this one as he was tagging their bags. Then he'd send the passengers on board, where they'd stand in the galley, their faces pressed to the cabin-door window, trying to spot the ground crew putting their bags in the belly of the plane.

When they didn't see this happen—and they can almost never see this happen—they'd demand that a flight attendant "go downstairs" and check that their bags made it.

Sometimes I'd pretend to do this. I'd sneak off to a lav or the cockpit, then return a few minutes later.

"A brown Samsonite?" I'd say and smile. "Oh yes, of course. It should be the first one off, too. No waiting in baggage claim for you!"

What could have been so important that this miniature woman tried to carry a bag that could carry her? It was Gary's fault, of course. He should have checked it. Mr. Hotlanta.

When I scanned the manifest, I found the woman's name. Mrs. Clemons. I brought Mrs. Clemons orange juice and a biscuit.

"Oh, I don't like to be trouble," Mrs. Clemons said.

"Thank you so much. It's my son, you see. He makes me fly up here. My son, he worries. I have arthur-itis and the bigger seats, well, he says it's better. My feet don't swell up as much if I've got some moving room. I don't like to be fussed over, though. I'm okay sitting in back. I tell him, 'I'm fine.' But ever since he's been in that band, he gets me these tickets and he says, 'Mama, you fly First Class; First Class for my mama.' I'm simple folk, but what can you do?

"My son, he plays horn. You like music?"

I nodded. She was wearing me down, and this time, when I smiled, I meant it.

"My son, he just loves playing horn. I always say, you have to find what you love in this world. Take you, for instance. You must love what you do, being so nice to help me and all. It's a blessing, Lord, it really is. A blessing."

I wanted to tell Mrs. Clemons about Ghislain, and about how I didn't believe that my job, on most days, had anything to do with being blessed. On most days, I'd have to say, although I loved parts of my life, I did not love what I had to do to get there. But Mrs. Clemons seemed so happy to talk with me about her son, so peaceful in this place where the call lights were going off like game-show buzzers and people all around us were scowling and checking their watches, that I kept this to myself.

As she went on, Mrs. Clemons, I realized, was making me feel better.

Not good, but better.

Some days, I found comfort in disappearing. Other days, like this one, I found comfort in being seen. I've given away free drinks, champagne, headphones—all the perks we were supposed to reserve for those times when we spill hot coffee on someone's lap or run out of meals or live through a bout of rougher-than-usual air—just because someone asked me how my day was going and waited for an answer.

This is why I wrapped up a bottle of red for Mrs. Clemons. I was sure she didn't drink. She might even have taken offense, but it was the best I had to offer, along with a few leftover chocolates. I hoped she'd take it and understand.

When she took the bottle, she said, "Oh, you shouldn't do this. You shouldn't fuss over me. But thank you. I don't know if it will fit in my bag, though. Gracious."

She laughed and patted me on the arm. "I'm going to tell my son how nice you've been. He worries, my son.

"He plays horn, like I said. I never much cared for rock 'n' roll myself, but it's been a blessing, really it has. He plays with this nice man, name of Bruce Springsteen. He's from New Jersey. You know him?"

Clarence Clemons. The Big Man. Mr. C. The Reverend CC.

In concert, Springsteen likes to tell about the time "the Big Man joined the band." It was, he says, an event of nearly biblical proportions that night when Clarence Clemons showed up during a storm and opened the door to the Student Prince Club, where Springsteen was playing for fifteen dollars a week on the boardwalk in Asbury Park.

The wind, Springsteen says, just blew the door off the hinges and Clarence stood there, lightning and thunder at his back, and said, "I'd like to sit in." They played "Spirit in the Night." Midway through the song, their eyes connected. They looked at each other, and that, Springsteen says, was that.

Clarence Clemons.

Tiny Mrs. Thelma Clemons's son.

All six foot three, three hundred pounds of him.

The Christmas after I met Mrs. Clemons, the *St. Petersburg Times* ran a story. The headline read, "An Angel Named Clarence." It was about Clarence's volunteer work with Jesus And You, or JAY, a crack-house-turned-mission on Avenue S in Riviera Beach, Palm Beach County's version of the inner city.

In the story, Clarence, along with Brother Bob Felder, the mission's founder, sat at a long table with residents and listened to their stories.

Henry Mason Jr. talked about the time he was shot in the stomach and came to JAY to heal so that he could kill the man who shot him.

"But instead," Mason said, "I healed my spirit and feel like I have a purpose in life now."

Jennifer Clayton said she used to be a hooker addicted to cocaine, and JAY helped her regain custody of her five children.

Bill Clark, who'd spent most of his forty-seven years in prison, touched Clarence's hand.

He said, "I used to listen to this man's music when I

was sitting in prison. This is something beyond my wildest dreams, to be an ex-con, a lifelong drug user, then to sit here at the same table with a world celebrity like Mr. Clemons."

Clarence told the reporter, Dave Scheiber, that he learned all about kindness and love from his parents, who were sometimes too poor to buy anything but comic books for their children for Christmas.

He said, "It only takes one person, a person to treat the problems from the inside out."

Scheiber called the mission a place "where many lives have been pulled back from the brink and rejuvenated." He said that Clemons made broken lives wonderful.

When the flight was over, I helped Mrs. Clemons with her bag. I walked her to the end of the jetway. I thanked her for flying with us, wished her a good day, and handed her off to a gate agent. Everything was the way it always was, and I doubt that Mrs. Clemons would have remembered me after that flight. I'm sure she told her stories to every flight attendant she met on every flight she was ever on. I'm sure she was always open and unassuming, and that she never thought about it much. But on that flight on that day, she may have just saved my life, and I would have liked to have told her that. Mrs. Thelma Clemons, who taught her son everything he knows about kindness.

carry on

He called me Honey.

He talked loud, wore a white cowboy shirt with red fringe across the chest. "Honey," he said. "Honey, I need to get to the bathroom."

It was dark, and I hadn't seen the hand that grabbed hold of my leg, though this wasn't unusual. I'd been a flight attendant long enough to get used to being touched like this.

I had to look hard to see the man, his round face lit by his reading light. Then it clicked. 22D. A preboard. A carry-on. That's what we call them, carry-ons, like luggage. He'd lost both legs. That's what we say. Lost.

This happened on the all-nighter, Vegas to New York, a rotation I worked whenever I could get it. I liked the hours. By the time I went to work at 11 PM, everyone I wanted to avoid on the ground was asleep. By the time I came home, they were on their way to work. Plus, there were the long layovers—at least twenty-four hours in hot, sunny weather—and, of course, the slot machines and blackjack tables I'd grown to love.

As for the route itself, the fares were cheap, but the

passengers were usually mean, particularly on the way back from losing all their savings.

On the way over, they drank until they passed out.

On the way back, we kept the lights down and hoped they'd all just leave us alone.

I knelt down next to the man, and said, "Sure, how can I help?"

I smiled and tried to look calm, casual. I'd been trained in blanket lifts, on-board wheelchairs, ways of preserving dignity in times like these. Still, I was afraid. The man was big, and I wasn't sure what I could do to help him.

He said I should just walk in front. He'd do the rest.

He'd already raised his armrest when I started to shake my head and explain to him that this wasn't how it was done, this was not regulation. If he'd wait, I'd get the wheelchair, I said. I'd get help. He smiled at me, nodded.

"I like to take care of things on my own," he said. "I've had a lot of practice." Then he lifted himself with his arms and lowered himself to the ground.

The carpet on an airplane is rough, industrial. It has to be to handle the things I'd seen strewn on it after a flight like this—used Kleenex, dirty diapers, full airsickness bags, wads of chewing gum, and a mélange of half-chewed pretzels, heel-ground peanuts, and spilled Scotch on the rocks.

Now here was this man, pulling himself along, all that filth and grit against his palms.

He wanted to chat, and paced his questions against the weight of his breathing, the effort of pulling himself down the long narrow aisle.

How long had I been flying?

Did I like my job?

He himself felt blessed every day he woke up. Blessed.

I kept trying to clear the way, bags and blankets everywhere, plastic casino cups, newspapers, jumbled shoes, arms and legs flopped out over the armrests.

Soon he would get some legs, he said. The doctors back home were making some for him, had to be customized, you know. He'd gotten some money together. He'd saved up. He'd planned to win the rest at Caesars but, well, you know.

He kept talking as he dragged himself through the aisle behind me, his head at armrest level, his torso pulled along behind him like a shell.

When we got to the lav, he grabbed hold of my arm. His hand was huge, like a mill worker's. He steadied himself between me and the wall, and my arm shook under the weight.

"It's okay," he said. "I just need you to wait here, then walk me back."

I watched him pull himself into the tiny stall, push against the door. I heard the thud of his body, the fumbling, and all I could think of was the lav floor, sticky with spilled soap and urine, and his face, moving through the cabin, brushing against the soles of strangers' shoes.

There are times in my life when I want to believe some of the things I learned as a girl—that people get only about as much as they can handle in this world, that suffering leads to a kind of otherworldly transcendence and enlightenment. But I don't think it's true, any of it. I think those are things we learn so that, later in life, we can justify our own good luck.

When he came out of the bathroom, he said, "Okay then. Ready?"

In the fluorescent light of the galley, I could see his eyes were very blue. The brows above them were thick and blond and curved like question marks. He had a sweet face, open, Midwestern.

He was wearing Wranglers, cut off and hemmed above the knees to fit, and a huge belt buckle. On the buckle, there was a bronze cartoon cowboy giving a fat thumbs-up. Beneath the cowboy were the words, KEEP ON TRUCKIN'.

I should have asked his name, where he was from. Instead, I asked the things I always ask to protect what was left of my heart.

"Did you like Vegas?"

"Wasn't the weather gorgeous?"

"Were you lucky?"

He laughed. "I come every year. You never know when it's going to be your time."

jackpot

A year after I started flying, I called my parents to say I was ready to quit the airlines. My mother said, "Let me put your father on the phone."

I knew something was up.

"What's wrong, honey?" my father said, stretching the syllables the way he used to when I was six and prone to crying jags over anything from Shaun Cassidy's love for that bimbo Deanie to a flat on my Barbie Country Camper.

"I think I've got to get out of this," I said. "I think I made a mistake."

What I didn't say was that, over the past few months in New York, I'd watched three guys with baseball bats beat a rat to death. A graffiti artist sprayed HUMPTY DUMPTY WAS PUSHED on the front of the hotel where I was staying. I was mugged by four kids on Rollerblades. They took my passport and my car keys. They called me "ma'am." One morning, I found a roach nibbling dried toothpaste off my toothbrush. My car had been broken into. Twice. A passenger had licked me—actually licked me—on the neck during a beverage service. Another passenger had thrown a salad, loaded with ranch dressing, at my butt.

I was not writing. My love life was, of course, in the toilet, although I suppose I had options. I could go to Paris. Or I could stay put, leave Diego, and take my chances on native romantic soil. I mean, I had prospects. After all, I'd been hit on again and again at 5 AM by Kenny The Cab Driver.

Kenny was about five feet tall and bald, except for a wiry ponytail at the base of his neck. He drove a gypsy cab in my neighborhood in Queens, and his rates for flight attendants were cheap because he figured he could get some action on the side. Kenny smelled like ear wax, his cab had a couple of bullet holes in the front passenger-side door, and his come-on line was "When you gonna give me some digits?"

I'd run over my childhood idol Walter Cronkite's foot with a beverage cart on the DC shuttle and left him limping off the plane, his little CBS News briefcase sagging off his shoulder.

I'd been called in to see my supervisor—not because of Mr. Cronkite's injuries, but because I'd been late to a flight. In her presence, I had to write on a piece of lined yellow paper:

I was late for a flight because I did not give myself enough time to make it to the airport. I was not being proactive. This will not happen again.

Then my supervisor, who was nearly six feet tall if you measured from the top of her updo, opened her bottom desk drawer. She took out a bottle of nail-polish remover and a cotton ball and gestured at my glittery pink fingertips.

"Your nail polish is not regulation," she said. "Please review the guidelines for Flight Attendant Makeup and Accessories. And choose a more flattering color next time."

"Things aren't really working out," I told my father.

There was a long pause, and I thought I heard my mother whispering something in the background. It was hard to be sure, because my father was jiggling the phone cord, making static on the line. The static was coming in waves and getting worse, like he was purposely trying to break the connection.

"Your mother wants to know . . . well . . . if you quit," my father said, "does that mean I can't go to Vegas when I want?"

My father had never asked me for anything in his life. But, like most parents of airline employees, he liked his flight privileges. More to the point, he liked Las Vegas. Since I'd started flying, he and my mother headed out west almost once a month.

They'd become regulars at the Pittsburgh airport. On their last trip, for instance, my father was stopped at Security. This, according to my mother, happened often. The guards made my father open his suspiciously heavy carry-on. They pulled out four old sweat socks loaded up with change and knotted shut with rubber bands.

"For the slots," my father explained.

"Oh, he's a real character all right," my mother fumed to me over the phone from their hotel later that night. "He's crazy. I told you he's crazy, he's always been crazy, and now everyone at that airport knows."

Crazy or not, my father had locked on to Las Vegas as his last ticket out, his final hope after he gave up on Broadway and Florida.

He didn't have many other choices. Like I said, he wasn't much for bingo.

"Too many old farts pissing and moaning," he'd say. "Forget about it. The smell of Ben-Gay makes me sick."

And he'd started to think about trading in his bookie for a financial adviser. "The stock market," he'd say. "Now there's a plan with a future."

His bookie, he'd decided, was crooked.

"I should be hitting, for Christ's sake," my father said. "It's fixed."

This was after my father gave up playing his usual losing round of house numbers and birthdays and began to consult a book he said should have given him an edge.

The Amazing Dream Book—which he'd ordered from a *Parade* magazine ad that said "Your Dreams Can Change Your Life!"—converted dream images into lucky numbers.

Whenever he had a particularly vivid dream, like the one he had about a big black dog carrying a yellow cat on its back across a river—my father would look the image up in *The Amazing Dream Book*.

First, the book would give the meaning of the dream. According to the book, a black dog is a good omen. It's good that the dog is large. That means you have a powerful protector. A cat is an unfortunate omen. It means you're facing a run of bad luck. Yellow is a good omen. It means good luck. Sunny days ahead. A river could be a good omen or a bad omen, depending on whether the water is muddy or clear.

Then the book would give advice.

In the case of my father's dream, the advice was: Take vitamins.

Finally, using "numerology of the Eastern, Western, and Pythagorean methods," the book would break down the dream into lucky lottery numbers. Black: 10, 14, 11. Dog: 14, 16, 17. Yellow: 25, 37, 29. Cat: 7, 9, 6. River: 16, 25, 36.

"It's a science. Really, it is," my father would say. And then he'd dial his bookie.

Me, I dreamed of airplanes. Usually they were crashing. According to the dream book, dreaming of airplanes means "you desire to rise above it all, escape." To dream of crashing means "a literal warning—avoid whatever it is that's crashing."

My lucky numbers were 26, 45, 40, 16, 21, and 22.

I didn't play the lottery. And I don't know what my birthday in a box for a dime or a series of divinely inspired dream digits in a box for a buck would get you, because my father hardly ever hit. So I've always been pretty sure he was banking on the stock market and Vegas to change his life.

Around the time I was thinking about quitting my job, my father had been investing more and more of his savings into the stock market. His prize stocks—Disney, Xerox, and Microsoft—were all down. Vegas, I'm sure, was more important to my father than ever.

When they were in Vegas, my parents stayed at The Lady Luck, a few blocks off the Strip. Their house was full of Lady Luck pens, miniature bottles of Lady Luck shampoo and Lady Luck hand cream, Lady Luck shoehorns, Lady Luck notepads, and Lady Luck shower caps.

"Good deal, nice people," my father said. "Treat you like you're something special."

My mother played the nickel slots, usually the first machines she saw, which meant the ones by the casino entrance.

"Those are the ones that hit because that way all the people see you win," my mother explained. "People think the casino's paying out when they see all those lights going off."

My father had a more spiritual method. He'd walk around, sweat sock stuffed into a plastic casino cup, and wait for a slot machine to call to him.

One year, my mother hit for five hundred dollars.

My father never hit at all.

"But I still don't lose," he'd say. "The casinos, they give you all sorts of free deals. Free chips, free drinks, free hot dogs with sauerkraut, free shrimp cocktail, nice hotel room, free shows. Beautiful. I always come out ahead."

There was a story going around right after I started flying. A new flight attendant on a Vegas layover put a dollar into a slot machine at the Hard Rock and hit the jackpot. If the story was right, we're talking one or two million dollars. She called Scheduling and told them they could go fuck themselves, that she wasn't working the flight back. Then she bought a First Class ticket on another airline home.

The flight attendant was a legend. She bought a house—cash. A Mercedes—cash. She got the boob job she'd always wanted. She'd never have to work again. Her story gave us all hope that, at any minute, our luck could turn and we could kiss everything we didn't love good-bye.

I'd told my dad that story, and he'd said, "That's what I'm talking about. That's it right there."

Like I said, my father never asked me for anything in his life.

"If you have to quit, quit then," he said. "That's that."

"I'm just talking, really," I said. "You know me. I'll stick it out for a while. Besides, I'm in New York, right? Greatest city in the world. Things will get better. Maybe I'll even get this pilot I know to teach us his secret to winning at craps. He's written this computer program and everything."

"Craps?" my father said. "Craps is for suckers."

What can you do?

Everyone who knows anything about gambling will tell you that, when it comes to Vegas, craps give you the best odds.

But that's how it was with my father. With me, too, for that matter. Neither one of us was what you'd call a natural-born winner. The best we could hope for was to stay in the game.

sexy nyc

I scribbled the address of the publishing company on the palm of my hand. Empire State Building. This interview was it, I was sure.

Despite my promise to my father, I was—in my heart, at least—done with the airlines and those fifteen-hour days of popping Diet Cokes until my index finger bled, racing to find airsickness bags and not making it in time, and playing referee between passengers who just couldn't get along.

If I could find the perfect job, in this, my perfect city, my father would understand. The New York life I pined for would be a reality. I'd be successful and buy my father First Class tickets to Vegas, after all.

Since I came to New York, all my dreams had been sidetracked. I'd forgotten my plans to find work as a writer or editor. My poetry didn't take off. I wasn't giving standing-room-only readings in hip coffeehouses. I hadn't been discovered by an agent who had connections at all the big publishing houses. After a while, I wasn't writing at all. Although I'd signed up for a workshop at the 92nd Street Y, I missed almost all the classes because I had to fly.

I choked on clove cigarettes and I didn't have the budget or the ankles for Manolo Blahniks. Instead of losing twenty pounds and reshaping myself into a svelte *That Girl* urbanite, I'd gained five pounds eating ramen noodles and huge greasy slices of New York pizza on my flight-attendant budget.

You must revise your life, William Stafford used to tell his students.

"I cannot waste time on what I do not love," Ghislain had told me.

"It's a blessing, really it is," Mrs. Clemons had said.

For me, all of this meant only one thing. I had to find a job on the ground.

As job searches went, I'd had half a dozen painfully unsuccessful interviews—at the Poetry Society of America, at the Academy of American Poets, even at Norton (no new career, no book contract, but a free and very uncomfortable pasta lunch at a swank restaurant near the Public Library). All secretarial positions. I type ninety words a minute, but my employment history includes stints as a university lecturer, a newspaper reporter, a public relations spinner. No administrative assisting, very little proof of my office skills. And then there was that master's degree in poetry. Plus I was working as a flight attendant. Prospective employers seemed suspicious.

Take this one woman, for instance—sad and pale, an otherworldly Prozac glaze to her eyes, gray hair clipped into a severe bob that sat precisely above the collar of her designer suit. She stopped in the middle of an interview for an entry-level position that paid eighteen thousand a year, no benefits, closed her notebook, put down her very expensive-looking pen, and said, "You don't want this job."

I said, "No, I do. I do want this job."

She said, "No, what I think you really want is my job. And you can't have my job."

I didn't know what to say to that.

I wanted to explain to her how miserable I was, how I wanted to do anything that had something to do with poetry and books and writers and the romanticized New York literary life I'd always imagined. I wanted to tell her I dreamed of a life in this city I'd always loved. I wanted to tell her the building she worked in was beautiful—couldn't she understand this?—that I was willing to be poor (hell, I was already poor) just so that I could walk through those beautiful heavy wood doors with the leaded-glass windows, climb the winding staircase with the brass banister worn alternately dull and shining, and sit all day in an office that smelled of book dust and lemon polish.

Most of all, I wanted to tell her I was tired. No more short calls to Newark—an hour to get from Queens to New Jersey, fifty-dollar cab ride, in uniform, hair and nails in regulation shape, for a quick and nightmarish turnaround rotation to Fort Lauderdale, where we'd serve stale turkey pastrami sandwiches with little packets of designer mustards.

Once, on one of these trips, an elderly woman launched one of those sandwiches at my head, shouting,

"*You* eat this crap." I told her that I did eat that crap. Most days, there wouldn't be time to eat at all during a trip, and then even those little sandwiches seemed delicious.

What I didn't say was that, since I made ten thousand a year and lived in New York, I would often stuff my carry-on bag full of those sandwiches and stale pretzels and Diet Cokes. This was, of course, against airline regulations. A TWA flight attendant was fired during my first year of flying. She was caught taking a carton of milk off the airplane. The incident made the national news, and the story was passed around by our supervisors like a mantra. And though all junior flight attendants live in fear of being caught with a bagful of pilfered peanuts or a couple of mini-bottles of Bailey's, corporate theft becomes an inevitable life raft, especially if you happen to be based somewhere like New York or Los Angeles.

As for the woman in the designer suit, the gatekeeper to an alternate future, I don't think she cared that I couldn't take my current life any longer. She didn't understand anything about drunk passengers, the monotony of seat belt demos, "Beef or Chicken? Red or White?" She didn't know the agony of nine-hour layovers in bug-infested hotel rooms somewhere in Indiana or Wisconsin.

And so I just stood up, and said, "Well, I don't want your job. But thanks."

Still, I hadn't given up hope.

I kept the résumés faxing, and plundered the *New York Times'* classifieds every Sunday. And so, when I got the call about the Empire State Building gig, I wasn't immediately jaded. Sure, I didn't recognize the name of the publishing house, didn't remember which ad had sparked my interest in the job, but the address was enough to make it desirable. This was my Vegas jackpot, the job that would turn it all around.

I imagined myself taking the E train to the Downtown 6 every morning, stopping at a corner deli for a light-and-sweet coffee in a white paper "I ❤ NEW YORK" cup, and taking the elevator to my office in one of the world's most legendary and romantic buildings.

The building, in fact, was so legendary in my mind that I never thought of it as a functioning office space, full of ordinary, workaday businesses. For me, it seemed more a movie set, the kind of place you entered—in costume, in makeup—and your life was instantly transformed. *King Kong, An Affair to Remember, Sleepless in Seattle.* The great ape, Cary Grant, Meg Ryan, and me.

"I'll be there. Two o'clock. Thursday. Yes. Thanks. Thanks very much," I told the woman on the phone. Her voice was deep and soothing. She seemed kind.

"One thing," she said before we hung up. "How do you feel about working with adult content?"

"Oh, I'm very liberal. Not a problem. No problem at all. Fine, fine."

I assured her that I had, after all, been the editor of a literary magazine back in grad school a few years before. We had done special issues speaking out against censorship, particularly against the exploits of one Senator Jesse

Helms. I liked to think of myself as not only liberal, but radically so. I didn't ask the woman what she meant by adult content. In fact, I didn't even think about it, I was that pleased with my own politics.

And so, Thursday came, and I took my trains. I stopped at a deli, bought a coffee, a sesame seed bagel, and a *Daily News*. I was early, so I hung around the lobby, taking in the art deco ambience and avoiding the eyes of the security guards. I was nervous. I didn't want to seem nervous. I didn't want to look like a tourist in this building full of tourists. With their communal air, their somber clothing, most fashionable, successful Manhattanites seem like subtle accessories—tiny diamond studs, a jaunty silk scarf a pair of classic pumps—worn by the city itself. After all my joyful days of blending in on New York streets, here in this legendary building, even in my black suit, I worried that I stuck out like a mismatched sock or a pair of silvery sandals in a snowstorm. Everything about me, I was sure, blared desperation.

I kept checking my reflection in anything that would show it to me—walls, windows, a steel beam. I picked and prodded at my hair, which I'd swept up in a loose *I'm liberal!* twist, and checked my teeth again and again for stray sesame seeds or lipstick.

At one forty-five, I found the elevators that would take me to my new life. After a quick phone call to my would-be employer, the security guards let me slip between the famous elevator doors and take the ragged ride up into what I hoped would soon be my new office.

The doors slid open and I entered a narrow hall lined with Robert Mapplethorpe prints—huge lilies, an image of a man's naked and muscular back. This was a good sign, I thought. I knew some things about Mapplethorpe, and I thought this would help with conversation during the interview. Jesse Helms hated Mapplethorpe, and the senator began his campaign against the NEA as a result of what he found to be "vulgar" homoerotic images in the photographer's art. I could talk endlessly about Helms, and felt this would help me fit in.

There was only one door at the end of the hall, and so I opened it. The receptionist, her burgundy-dyed hair pulled back and waxed into the kind of high, heavy ponytail that gave me migraines as a child, had a phone balanced between her ear and her bony right shoulder as she sat at her desk, typing. She acknowledged my presence with a quick wave of her left hand, which indicated I should sit down in one of the two chairs that were pushed against the far wall of the room. The room was tiny and run-down. There were no magazines to read, nothing to distract. The chairs faced the receptionist, and after five minutes or so, I felt myself glazing over and staring at her as if she were on TV.

When she finally hung up the phone, she said, "You must be our two o'clock. Kathy will be with you in a few."

I smiled, nodded, nodded again. She smiled back, a crooked smile, off center, the kind of smile people sometimes give to lunatics, the kind of smile that says *Whoa there, okay, just relax*. Then she went on typing.

At two thirty, Kathy came for me. She was a large woman, solid. She wore a man's tie and suspenders with cartoon figures emblazoned on them—tiny Porky Pigs, Yosemite Sams, and Bugs Bunnies danced over her large breasts and wide shoulders. I thought she was going for a pop-culture Charlie Chaplin look, and that she must have a porkpie hat hanging on a hook on the back of her office door. Her voice was deep and throaty, the voice I recognized from the phone.

"Sorry you've been waiting," she said. "Come on back."

She led me through a tight maze of tiny cubicles and a few more Mapplethorpe prints, then into her office. Her desk was piled high with paper. Her computer was decorated with various animals made from pom-poms and attached to the top and sides of the machine courtesy of sticky, oversize, humanish feet.

"Let's see. You're a writer. You're looking for editorial work, correct?" Kathy said. She leaned back in her chair and it squeaked under her weight. She tucked her hands under her suspenders, and reminded me of a cheesy film-noir detective.

"Yes, that's right. Yes." I leaned forward. I wanted to look eager, but I probably looked like I'd just received an electric shock.

"Well, your background is impressive. The position we have open, though, is entry level. How do you feel about that?"

I muttered some things about wanting to learn the business, paying my dues, blah blah blah.

Kathy nodded. "And we talked about the issue of adult content?"

I spieled—liberal, anticensorship, blah blah blah.

"Well, good, then—so you could work on something like this?"

She opened the top drawer of her desk and pulled out three magazines. She fanned them out in front of me. The magazines were glossy, their names uniformly blasted out in bold type. The magazines had simple, direct names—*Sexy NYC*; *Legs, Legs, Legs*; and *Suck Me*.

I tried not to let anything register on my face.

"Sure, sure, no problem," I said. I didn't touch the magazines.

"Well," she said, "you might want to take a look at them just to get a feel for what we do."

I picked up one of the magazines and leafed my way to the centerfold. A woman in a black fishnet crotchless bodysuit was bent over, back to the camera, her wrists bicycle-chained to her ankles, which teetered on see-through Cinderella stilettos. The woman's face was mostly obscured, but her long dark hair hung down onto the floor, which looked wet and industrial.

The centerfold was part of a photo essay, Kathy explained, shot in the meatpacking district.

"Um, okay, yes, sure," I said, nodding.

I should say here that I have nothing against pornography. I have leafed through my share of *Hustler*s, *Playboy*s, and *Playgirl*s. I've rented porno flicks and learned to give head while watching *Flashpants* at a drive-in in the 1980s. I like erotica. I like sex toys. I've enjoyed window-shopping in Amsterdam's red-light district.

So what was the problem?

"What you'd be doing mostly is writing captions for photo essays like this one," Kathy was saying. "Do you think that would be something you'd be interested in doing?"

I nodded, and for a moment, believed it. At least the job would be challenging. I'd have to be creative, really push the envelope. It would be better than serving peanuts and Cokes and cleaning up an airplane lav after a bout of turbulence.

And then Kathy handed me a take-home assignment: a series of captionless black-and-white photocopied pictures. In the first one, a woman in large glasses and a lab coat was holding an empty test tube. As the series moved along, she lost the lab coat, the glasses, her hairpins, her regulation nursing shoes, and so on. For some reason, she held on to the test tube, even in the last spread-eagle shot.

I felt my writerly neurons click on despite themselves— *Why the test tube? What's the story here? Where are we going with this? Is this lab woman a sympathetic character?*

"Just take this home, write the captions, then fax it back to me by tomorrow," Kathy was saying.

My reverie crumpled.

Fax it.

Fax it? Where?

Tomorrow, if everything went on schedule, I'd land in

Kansas City at 10 PM. I imagined myself walking into an all-night Kinko's and handing over my project to an elderly clerk who would remind me of my sixth-grade music teacher. I imagined trying to fax it from the airport flight-attendant lounge. A perfect Barbie-esque supervisor would surely creep up behind me, tap me on my uniformed shoulder with her press-on French-manicured nails.

"We don't ah-prove of such thangs hare at our airline," she'd say, in a sugary accent.

Then she'd take me by the ear into her office and set my passport and employee ID on fire.

My heart took a titanic dive. So this is what it came down to. Even when I was willing to sell out, I didn't have it in me to let anyone else know it.

I thanked Kathy and put the photos in my bag.

"Oh, and you might want to take these along for inspiration," she said, smiling. She pushed the magazines toward me. Her hands, I noticed, were thick and masculine, the nails ground down and bare.

"Of course," I said. I grabbed at the magazines and stuffed them in my shoulder bag. "Thanks again. I'll have something for you tomorrow."

I shook her hand. I backed toward the door. I let myself out through the maze of Mapplethorpes, down the legendary elevators, and out onto the street, where I nearly knocked over a vending cart filled with hot peanuts.

I walked, block after block, and never felt so low. I knew I could get this job if I wanted it. I hated flying. I'd been looking for "editorial work," after all.

Mostly, I felt sick.

"Distracting," I could imagine Ghislain saying. "Leave the pornography to other people."

But what were my choices? In twenty-four hours, I'd be on my way, a three-day trip, four legs a day, full flights, with short layovers in Kansas City and Little Rock. The magazines in my bag seemed more promising than that. At least I'd be writing.

On my way to the subway, I stopped by the library. I wanted to check out some videotapes—a documentary on Walt Whitman and a Lannon interview with Allen Ginsberg. Now, there were two New York writers who, if they wrote porn, did it on their own time and never for a salary. I'd seen both videos before, but I needed a little inspiration. I planned to go home and open a bottle of wine one of my roommates had scored for me during a recent Paris run. I'd watch the videos, get drunk and weepy.

I checked out the tapes and headed for the exit. As I passed through the theft detectors, a guard—a huge grim-faced man who looked like George Foreman before he did muffler commercials and sold grills—touched my arm.

"Miss," he said. "Could you open your bag?"

I just stood there, watching his lips move over his large white teeth. *No hablo ingles.*

"Miss, your bag."

He pointed and I stared at the eel-like muscles of his arm, his meaty hands.

Slowly, I unzipped the bag.

There, on top, was my complimentary copy of *Suck Me*. On the cover was an image of a man, eyes ecstatically closed, his face content as a breast-feeding baby's, running his tongue between the toes of a perfectly pedicured foot, the little seashell-y nails tipped blood red, the ivory ankle cocked in delight, and, above it all, a woman's disembodied fingers dangling a pair of strappy spike-heeled red sandals that were, I'm sure of it, Blahniks.

my life in translation

Like my father, I always believed happiness was off the next exit ramp, in the next time zone, or just one continent over. Now that I'd had the chance to look for happiness just about everywhere in the world, I was still, for the most part, an impossible crank.

Bless Sheldon. Instead of laying over in Kansas City the day after the porn interview, I got a Stockholm trip. And so, instead of pulling the covers over my head in Kansas, I was in bed in the land of fish eggs, undercooked potatoes, and overpriced vodka.

Was I happy? Was I grateful and rethinking my life plans?

Hell, no.

My back ached. My feet looked like two veiny cream puffs that refused to be stuffed into my very American/Taiwanese Nikes. Eight hours of cabin pressure had made my face break out and given me a nasty case of jet belly, a condition that offers the worst symptoms of beer bloat and PMS and makes even male flight attendants look like they're in their second trimester.

I'd never been to Sweden before, and I was relieved to get Sheldon's call. I figured the chocolates I'd sent him the last time I was in Brussels had finally paid off. I called Trish back home in Pittsburgh with the news and she said, "Sweden? Good for you. Send a postcard. And bring me some caviar and a box of those gummy fish."

Now all I wanted to see was the bathtub and the bed here in the Provobis Hotel, where I triple-locked the door to this room done up in sherbet, all Swedish-hipster oranges and limes.

According to the hotel guest book, there was a palace, a shipwreck museum, cafés, and fresh salmon just down the street. But I had burned my right hand dishing out salmon in Business Class, where most of the passengers barely glanced up as I poured champagne for hours and scooped up their trash, and this had ruined both my appetite and my mood.

I didn't want to talk to anyone in any language, not even in a restaurant, not even to ask where the bathroom was. Especially not to ask where the bathroom was.

All I wanted was to stay in Room 1818 alone. There was international CNN and free Swedish porn on the TV—homework just in case I wanted to write those captions after all. And although the porn stars—all blond, all beautiful—did not speak English and there were no subtitles, some things never needed translation and for that, at least, I was glad.

I was tired, that's all. I was tired of thinking of language, how to say please, thank you, beer, wine, red or white, and good-bye in Swedish, French, German, and Polish.

I was tired of the international flight attendants in the lounge at JFK, the way they kissed hello—both cheeks, not one. One cheek is New York style and something I'd grown to like. One cheek says, *Hey, stranger, good to see we're in this together.* Two cheeks equal the kiss of death in *The Godfather.*

And I wished Al Pacino would send them to swim with the fishes, those sky divas, with their fake Gucci bags and thick accents, who said perpetually world-weary things like *Darlings, I'm doing Paris again this month and the room service is just dreadful.*

I hated the way they gossiped in languages other than English and the way you could tell it was gossip by the arch of their waxed and penciled-in eyebrows, the little flicking motions they made with their pinkies as if dispatching gnats.

I know this sounds ridiculous, because most of my friends are from Ireland, Argentina, France, Pittsburgh, and Ohio. Besides, I've always liked gossip. I liked to practice my Spanish in Associated Foods on Metropolitan Avenue in Queens, and my favorite pastime whenever I was in Barcelona, Spain, was to visit La Pipa club and sit with the bartender and take turns making up insults that worked in both Spanish and English.

My crowning achievement to date is still: *Usted es un dedo peludo, gordo y grande.*

The translation: You are a big fat hairy toe.

And so there I was, world-weary me, sad in Stockholm, stewing about a conversation I had with Anzia, a sweet Warsaw-based flight attendant, on the way over.

Anzia had made small talk on the jumpseat, asking about my name.

"Jakiela is Polish?" she said, but I didn't feel like explaining my complicated heritage, that my adopted father is Polish, that his parents came over on the boat, as we say, and that because he was ashamed of this he taught me only a few syllables of Polish, enough to get by with my grandfather, *dziadek*, who didn't speak English.

My Polish vocabulary consists of *dziekocham*, I love you, and *dziekuje*, thank you, *dobranoc*, good night, *piwo*, beer, *dupa*, ass, and *sto lat*, may you live one hundred years. My Polish word power, if fully engaged, let me make sentences like: "Thank you, beer, I love you; and good night, my ass—may you live one hundred years."

This is why I never spoke a full sentence to my grandfather. Whenever I had to talk to him, I'd use individual words, with the exception of *dupa*, and fill in the blanks with English, hoping he could understand. Even when I was very young, I wondered why I bothered.

My grandfather must have known I didn't love him, per se. We were strangers. We didn't speak each other's language and I saw him only out of my father's obligation, which meant occasional weekends and holidays. Although *thank you* and *good night* were useful, I didn't need to ask him about beer, which he always drank delicately, just as Sister Joseph did, from a juice glass. When he sneezed or drank, he didn't need my wishes for long life because he already seemed as ancient as a statue in the Carnegie. I don't remember ever seeing him move.

Whenever we went for a visit, my grandfather would be in the same spot, in a brown overstuffed recliner, where we'd left him last week or last month. The recliner, like all the furniture in his old gray house on Cherry Way in Braddock, Pennsylvania, was covered in plastic. The plastic was to protect from bodily oils, spilled beer or Kool-Aid, and the graphite carried into the house from Edgar Thompson Works, the steel mill down the street where my grandfather and some of his sons once worked. Whenever anyone would sit or stand in that living room, there would be the squeaking sucking sound of plastic on skin.

This is all I remember of my grandfather, who died when I was twelve. This, and the picture of Jesus's Sacred Heart that hung on the wall above his recliner. My grandfather would sit, speaking his loud indecipherable Polish, a juice glass of Iron City in his hand, under a Technicolor picture of Jesus with his chest split open like the frogs we'd dissect in school.

Jesus's heart was plopped in his right hand. It was wrapped in thorns and it dripped blood that burned like gasoline. Otherwise, the heart seemed anatomically correct, all the auricles and ventricles and arteries drawn with a doctor's-office precision that made the picture all the more terrifying.

It's no wonder I was always scared to visit my grandfather, although my mother and father both said he was a kind man. Once inside the house, I'd keep quiet and eat too much cheese—cubes of Swiss or Velveeta speared with tinsel-topped toothpicks. On Christmas and Easter, I'd gobble packs of holy wafers imprinted with pictures of lambs and angels, and then throw up on the way home.

I didn't tell Anzia any of this.

What I said was, "Jakiela? It's American," and I didn't even care that I was rude.

Americans, my friend Sinead says, are often rude. Americans, Sinead says, always want to be something they're not.

Sinead is from Galway, Ireland. Her grandfather was the driver for Michael Collins, the founding leader of the IRA. Sinead is sweet, and so she doesn't talk about this much, but I know she doesn't like American tourists, especially the ones who come to town with their American Express cards, green T-shirts and tennis shoes, and get in fights because the bars close too early.

When I told her my birth name, Phelan, I said, "I'm part Irish."

She was kind—Sinead is always kind—but she said, "Well, no, you're All American, like McDonald's." Then she bought me a drink coaster at a gift shop at the Bern, where all the tour guides are British. The coaster was made of laminated corkboard and imprinted with the Phelan family crest.

"In Gaelic, you know, Phelan means wolf," Sinead said.

I told her I'd learned this from a book back when I was in elementary school.

"But have you thought about it, really?" she said. "Wolf. It means you're fierce, but easily domesticated. You're also prone to fleas."

Since I'd started flying, I learned that the two most recognized words in the world are *Coke* and *okay*. It's important to remember not to accompany the latter with the traditional American hand motion—index finger to thumb, other three fingers raised like peacock feathers—which means *Okay, fuck you, asshole* in most other cultures.

In some countries, to wave good-bye you turn your hand around and wave hello to yourself.

The more I saw of the world, the more I wondered how anyone got along with anyone. This is why sometimes, even on good layovers like the Stockholm one, I went to my hotel room and didn't come out.

On the airplane, there were always fights. The fights usually, though not always, involved alcohol.

About three hours into the Stockholm flight, I had to cut two guys off. They were Swedes in coach, and they were drunk on the miniature vodkas they'd been stockpiling in their seat backs.

If you want to get drunk on an airplane, the trick is to get a drink from every flight attendant on board. That way no one keeps track. And it's good to be drunk on an airplane. It passes the time, makes you forget about the fact that you're trapped like a veal calf. It helps you sleep. The trouble is, you must be a good drunk, a mannered drunk, or you could be considered a federal offense.

Me, I never liked to cut anyone off. I think people

should have whatever joy they can find, however they can get it.

Back in Pittsburgh, I loved to drink in Dee's Bar on the South Side on Sunday afternoons with all the old men. You could get drunk for five dollars and spend the rest of your money in the jukebox, which looks like a character from *Lost in Space* and lets you download any song you've ever loved.

On a usual afternoon, I would spend five dollars on drinks, five dollars on tips, and ten dollars playing the Jim Carroll Band's "People Who Died."

In New York, I was a regular at Yer Man's Irish Pub on Metropolitan Avenue in Kew Gardens, also known as Crew Gardens because of all the flight attendants and pilots who live there. At Yer Man's, most of the bartenders were from Dublin. They had Sinead's great sense of irony and humor. They were beautiful and tragic. They argued over soccer and politics. They fell in love every night. And they gave airline people most of our drinks for free.

On the Stockholm flight, these Swedish guys on the plane were already drunk, and we had hours to go. They were getting loud, and when this happens, other passengers start to write down the names printed on flight attendants' wings if we don't do anything. And sometimes, of course, the drunks, they turn on you, and then we have to use these handcuffs that look like the ties for garbage bags, and really, who wants that?

So when these guys asked me for the next round, I had to lean over. I had to say, "I can offer you a Coke." And although they didn't speak much English, they understood the universal language of cola.

One of them looked like a young Einstein—his hair was wrecked and he had these big droopy eyes. I like to think about Einstein, the way he said we could all simplify our lives by not wasting our minds on things that don't matter. Einstein had a closet full of identical suits, shirts, and shoes. He didn't remember his own phone number because he could always look it up.

This one, the young Einstein, said, "Sorry," and, "Vodka is expensive in Sweden, government prices," and "We just are happy to go home."

What can you do?

They slept for most of the flight. They were polite and seemed kind. Before we landed, I packed an airsickness bag full of all the vodka we had left in Coach and gave it to them.

It wasn't much. A few miniature bottles of Absolut and Stolichnaya, but I hoped it was enough for a little post-flight party. I hoped they drank it up on the spot. I hoped they toasted each other in their native land, in their native tongue. I hoped whatever they said to each other—*sto lat, vivir, ching ching, to life*—was as clear as the obnoxious sunshine that wouldn't let up all day.

you're looking at a miracle

When he was feeling gruff, one of my father's jabs was:
"Wake up and face reality. You're living in a dream world,
kid."

I hated this. The words now, compared to a lot of
things my father said over the years, seem pretty soft, but
back when I was growing up, they felt bitterly cruel. I
knew my father had stopped living in a dream world years
ago, and I'd seen what happened to him. I wanted to hold
out as long as possible, maybe because I knew even then
that we all eventually wake up, whether we want to or not.

Somewhere between that Stockholm trip and the night
I got the phone call from my mother saying that my father
was sick, I'd started to realize my dream was over.

"He's talking in his sleep, in Polish," my mother told
me on the phone. "He's not right. I just don't know."

My mother hadn't worked full time since she married
my father, but she practiced her nursing at home and
sometimes worked weekends at Braddock General. As a
child, I knew all the clinical words for body parts and dis-
eases. I never had colds. I had upper respiratory infections.

I did not have a belly button. I had an umbilicus. My mother read the *Physicians' Desk Reference* the way her friends read cookbooks. She diagnosed every sniff and cough.

I had to admit, she was good.

And now, where my father was concerned, she was worried.

A month earlier, on a visit back home, I could see he'd lost weight, even though his appetite, especially for things like chocolate snack cakes and ice cream, was huge. He had a pain in his back that seemed to be getting worse. He had a huge black mole on his neck that he scratched until it bled.

This was around the time my father had that dream about the dog carrying the yellow cat across the river. Despite *The Amazing Dream Book*'s assurance that he simply needed vitamins and a sequence of winning numbers to get his life back on course, my mother, the trained medical professional, was superstitious, too. She believed she had psychic powers, and was sure the dream was an omen.

"He didn't tell you Mitch Paitch was in that dream, did he?" my mother said.

Mitch Paitch was a name I hadn't heard in years. He was one of my father's few friends from the old neighborhood—someone who remembered when my father drank and sang and dressed up in suits to take my mother dancing.

I remember Mitch Paitch and my father one night on our porch. I'm not sure how old I was, but I was in the yard, trying as usual to fill a mayonnaise jar with lightning bugs. Citronella candles burned on the window ledges. They didn't do much for the mosquitoes, but they were the only source of light other than the red tip of my father's cigarette, which bobbed and glowed as the two men tried out a few bars of a song I didn't know.

"Christ, Paitch," my father said. "What are you, deaf?"

"Look who's talking," Mitch said. "Those cigarettes are killing you."

Mitch Paitch died decades ago. My father never talked about him. My mother lost touch with his wife.

"It's strange for him to just show up," my mother said. "It's not good, I can tell you that."

My mother planned to take my father to the doctor early the following week. I had a week off, and planned to spend it in Paris. I was not going to see Ghislain. I was taking Diego. This, of course, was a mistake, but at the time it seemed like a good idea. I could hear my father in me— *I can really breathe in Paris.* I was sure I'd be happy there, and that maybe things with Diego would finally be as romantic and good as I imagined.

Ghislain had been right after all. I'd known this from layovers and an earlier visit I'd taken with my parents a year before, but it still amazed me: Paris is the most beautiful city in the world. At the Eiffel Tower, I stood on the observation deck with my head literally in the clouds, almost eye level with the small tourist planes that circled the city. Paris is a dream. With Diego, however, it was not a good one.

He'd made an itinerary for us to follow. The highlight included visiting the catacombs, those famous miles of tunnels filled with the bones of plague victims and fallen revolutionaries. At the entrance to the catacombs, there is a sign that warns visitors not to take human remains for souvenirs. Inside, Diego fingered bullet holes in skulls and tested the sharp edges of shattered leg bones. He took pictures.

"Smile," he said as he made me pose in front of a huge mound of skulls arranged to look like a heart. "Isn't it romantic?"

It was, finally, too much.

Like my mother, I believed in omens, too.

Back in New York, there was a message from my father on my answering machine.

"Lori, this is your dad. Call me. I've got the damnedest thing to tell you. Call me. This is Dad."

It turned out that my father was scheduled for back surgery.

"Get this," he said when I called back. "It's a disc problem. A goddamn disc. The doctors say they usually see this in young men. Never men my age. I told you. I'm going to live to a hundred. I'm going to be around. Hell, my back doesn't even know how old it is."

When my mother got on the phone, she said, "I don't know. I just don't know."

The next day, I said to Diego, "I don't think we should see each other for a while."

"You don't mean that," he said.

Then I took a flight home to Pittsburgh.

I'd worked that morning, so I was still in my uniform, wheeling my squeaky roll-aboard, which left a black trail on Forbes Hospital's just-waxed linoleum. When I entered the waiting room, my mother saw me and began to cry. She'd been right, of course. When the doctors opened up my father, they found cancer, not a disc problem. The cancer had spread from his lungs to his spine. The liver, the doctors said, was involved. The brain, too.

"He's still unconscious," my mother said. "He doesn't know."

She and I were there when he woke up, groggy from the drugs, but still proud because he believed he was suffering from a young man's disease.

"The damnedest thing," he said and smiled at me. "Damnedest thing."

I can't remember how much time passed before he was fully conscious, before I had to tell him what had gone wrong. My mother couldn't do it, and I didn't want it left to the doctors.

"Dad," I said. "It wasn't a disc."

He didn't believe me. He didn't believe the doctors at first when they came in with their charts and diagnoses and treatment plans. He made a nurse write the words "metastasized adenocarcinoma, both lungs" on a piece of paper. He looked at the paper, with its clip-art heart and ad for a new blood pressure drug, then folded it into a neat square.

"Put that in my wallet," he said, and I did. Later, after

he died, my mother would find it there, tucked behind his driver's license.

In the hospital room, my mother wanted to know how long my father would live. She pulled the doctors aside. They hedged. Finally, she cornered one of the nurses.

"I know you know," my mother said. "I'm a nurse. Tell me. How long?"

"We can't be sure, we can never be sure," the nurse said.

"How long?" my mother said.

"Usually a year," the nurse said, and looked away.

From that point, I commuted between New York and Pittsburgh. Some days I woke up in hotel rooms. Some days I woke up in my pink childhood bedroom back in Trafford. Some days, if my father had a bad night, I woke up on a small sofa next to the hospital bed in my mother's old sewing room, listening to my father breathing.

My world started to shrink down to small spaces—an airplane cabin, the low ceilings and tiny rooms in my parents' house, a taxicab, my single bed in my apartment in New York, a hotel bathtub. Whatever sense of time or place I'd had was gone. My life had become one long series of flights, this city, that city, time zones, datelines, until I never was quite sure where or even who I was.

If I was away for a week, I'd come home to find my father changed. He took chemo cocktails and radiation treatments. There were more and more pills for my mother to look up in *Physicians' Desk Reference*. Each time, I wasn't sure what to expect when I'd ring my parents' doorbell and wait for the door with all its chain locks and bolts to finally swing open.

A few weeks into chemo, my father started wearing an old knit cap he'd kept from his navy days. He'd worn that cap as a crew member on the *Lexington*, a World War II aircraft carrier that had been in the Pacific. That cap and my father had survived kamikazes and air strikes and storms at sea. It didn't matter that it was now spring, that western Pennsylvania humidity had already started to set in. When I pulled up one day in a taxi, there was my father, under the hood of his Chrysler, that blue knit cap pulled down over his eyebrows. He was wearing his old work clothes, a uniform I thought had retired with him after he left his job at Radform.

He barely looked up. "Your mother's inside," he said.

"What's with the hat?" I asked my mother, who was bent over the sink, peeling carrots and potatoes for a pork roast, one of the few things my father still wanted to eat.

"His hair," she said. "He's upset about his hair."

When he was young, my father had that wavy Jacques Brel hair, sans bowl cut, but it had been gone for years. My father, his brothers, and most of the old Polish men I knew in Pittsburgh, looked like the pope. They were almost completely bald, except for the spiderweb strands of white hair they'd let grow long, then wear in comb-overs across the tops of their heads. My father, in his last gesture of vanity, always carried a comb in his back pocket. I think he secretly borrowed my mother's hairspray or dollops of her pink Dippity-do hair gel, because his strands always stayed in place.

That night, I never saw my father without that hat. He wore it through dinner when he picked at the tiny piece of roast on his plate. He wore it to watch the news. He wore it when he fell asleep on the couch. He wore it when my mother took him to bed. When I woke the next morning, there it was.

He never said anything about it to me and I didn't say anything about it to him.

I said, "How are you feeling, Dad?"

"What do you think?" he said. "Like shit. They're poisoning me."

And that was that. On the kitchen table, I noticed a blue prayer book and news clippings neighbors had cut from *Parade* magazine and *Reader's Digest*. There were handwritten notes—"Get well"; "Take care"; "Try this— my sister did and it works"—next to headlines touting the latest cancer miracle cures.

When my father was setting up a fallout shelter in our basement back in the early 1970s, he mail-ordered a bottle of Minutemen Survival Tablets ("A compact, lightweight, lifesaving food ration for any emergency") and a huge bag of apricot pits. The survival tablets he stored in the basement. The apricot pits he kept in the refrigerator. The pits tasted like wads of bitter sawdust. My father ate them every night. They were supposed to have a trace of something awful in them—cyanide, I think. According to an ad in *The Liberty Lobby*, that's what warded off cancer.

"Kills the bad cells," my father said back then as he munched on a handful of pits, then washed them down with milk. "Those corrupt FDA bastards won't okay laetrile—have to go to Mexico for that. But they can't make apricot pits illegal."

When I opened my parents' refrigerator on my first few commutes home, I expected to see another bag of apricot pits, but my father had given up on them long ago.

"A scam," he said. "Corrupt."

What I didn't see in the refrigerator, or anywhere in the house for that matter, were cigarettes.

"He quit," my mother said. "Just like that."

"I'm going to beat this," my father said. "They're not going to kill me off that easy, the cockroaches."

The cockroaches this time around were the doctors. One, in particular, had made my father furious.

"Do you know what he said to me?" my father said. We were sitting on the couch, watching *60 Minutes*. My father had on his blue cap. He looked at the TV while he talked. "He said, 'How old are you? Seventy-five?' He said, 'You lived your life.' Now what the hell kind of thing is that to say?"

I didn't say anything. I didn't know what to say. My father looked at me then, straight on, in a way he hadn't done in years.

"I'm dying, you know," he said.

"Yes, Dad, I know," I said.

"Okay, then," he said.

Neither of us said anything more after that.

It was hard to find a place to be alone in my parents' house, so I waited until my father went to bed. Then I went down to the basement, where years ago he'd put in a small bathroom and a shower stall so he could take showers after work without tracking graphite through the house. I took a shower, then sat on the floor of the stall. Sure that my parents wouldn't be able to hear, I broke down and finally wept.

Each time I'd come and go, I noticed that my mother was changing, too. She looked older, tired. She wore sweat suits in cheerful purples and pinks, but her face was pale. She put on makeup only when she and my father went to church on Sunday. She stopped curling her hair. She started taking my father's sleeping pills—she'd checked them out in *Physicians' Desk Reference* and said they weren't addictive—but then she was afraid she'd sleep too soundly, so she stopped. She started to be afraid.

"He's just so angry," she said.

Long distance, she told me she'd made my father sell his gun.

"What gun?" I said. My high school boyfriend once told me that my father had mentioned a gun to him, but I'd thought it was a joke, a fake threat to keep my boyfriend in line.

"He's had it since the war. Didn't you know?" my mother said. "He never kept bullets in it. He kept it hidden in the attic. But now, I don't want him near it. He thinks everyone's out to get him. Who knows what he might do."

She told me she stopped going to cardiac rehab because my father was convinced she was having an affair with her thirty-year-old trainer. When he heard my father was sick, the trainer had sent my mother a card. The card said, "Thinking of You." My father went crazy. He called the trainer and told him to stay away from my mother or else. He ripped up the card, then pulled the pieces from the trash, taped them together, and hid them in his sock drawer.

"I've got evidence," my father told me on the phone. "You don't know what she's like."

"He's crazy," my mother whispered. "It's in his brain."

"I'll be home this weekend," I said.

The doctors intensified the chemo treatments and the radiation. My father's face and chest were covered with burns. He looked like he could die any day.

Then he went into remission.

This was August, around my mother's birthday. I came home and took my parents to dinner to celebrate. They picked Red Lobster, the best seafood you could get within ten miles of Trafford. My mother and I drank wine. We all ordered Admiral's Feasts and extra orders of fried shrimp. Fried shrimp always reminded my parents of when they were first dating. My father would splurge and stop by Eat 'n' Park before he'd pick up my mother. He'd show up at her door dressed like a mobster, with a basket of shrimp in one hand and a strawberry pie in the other.

"That shrimp was the size of baby fists," my mother said.

"Can't get shrimp like that anymore," my father said.

At Red Lobster, we ordered dessert. The waitstaff came and sang "Happy Birthday," complete with hand claps and a line dance, for my mother. My father ate everything. He was glad to have an appetite. He ate his cake and my mother's.

"It's too good to waste," he said.

When the waitress brought the check, my father grabbed her hand. She was probably forty, with a long ponytail, flaking mascara, and the tired patience of someone who'd been waiting tables a long time.

"You're looking at a miracle," my father told her. "I should be dead. I'm not. God cured me. I'm here for my wife's birthday. It's a goddamn miracle."

When my father wouldn't let go of her hand, the waitress patted his shoulder with that *there, there* gesture of comfort we all know. She said, "God bless you, darling. Good for you." Then she wriggled free.

After that, I went back to New York and stayed away from Pittsburgh for a few weeks. I tried to get my life back into a rhythm and I spent time alone on my days off. I was happy to melt into the city again, where I could disappear, where nothing was expected of me. I hung out at the dog run in Washington Square Park, or drank wine and read the *Times* at my usual table at Café Tina. I wandered around the Museum of Art and just sat in the sculpture room, marveling at Rodin. From biographies and films, I knew that Rodin had been a horrible bastard to anyone who ever loved him. Still, he had to know so much about the body, about what it meant to be human, to be able to sculpt like that—all those lovely tortured faces, the marble veins that seemed full of blood.

I kept in touch with my parents every day on the phone. Things seemed to be going well. My father was upbeat.

"I feel strong," he said. "Screw those doctors. What do they know?"

"Who knows?" my mother said. "We're making plans, a few little trips here and there. Your father, he wants to go to Vegas."

I kept working, happier than ever for the escape, the empty hotel rooms, the big beds, other flight attendants to talk to on the jumpseat, the chance to not have to talk at all.

It didn't last long, maybe two months. Then the tumors in my father's brain flared. My mother had suspected this before the doctors confirmed it. She was sure on the morning she and my father were to leave for Vegas.

I found out about all of this in a hotel in Washington, DC. I was in the middle of a trip, a three-day shuttle rotation. I'd been holed up in my room, watching *The X-Files*, when the phone rang.

"He insisted on driving," my mother said. "Stubborn jackass."

Her voice was deep and thick. I could tell she'd been crying.

For days beforehand, my father had been losing his balance. He didn't tell anyone, but my mother saw him fall in the driveway. He'd been working on the Chrysler, trying to check the oil, when he stood up, wobbled, and went down.

"Nearly hit his head on the concrete," she said.

For whatever reason, my mother let my father bully her into not canceling their Vegas plans.

"I need to get away," he said.

At five o'clock the morning of their flight, my father got behind the wheel. My mother climbed into the passenger seat. She was a nervous passenger on a good day; I could see her holding on to the Chrysler's huge dashboard, her foot on an imaginary brake, as my father swerved along the parkway, going on and off the road, in and out of his lane.

When they got to the airport, my father discovered that his wallet was missing. My father had never, in the nearly fifty years that my mother had known him, forgotten his wallet. He was obsessive about it, always patting his hip pocket to be sure his wallet was where it should be. And yet he had left home for this trip without it. My mother took this as a cosmic sign that they weren't meant to get on that plane.

And so they turned around and came home.

"It was a miracle," my mother said. "A miracle. When we got home, the wallet was right there on the kitchen table. Had we gotten on that plane, I don't know what would have happened. We made it home. We got him home. A miracle. The doctor wants me to bring him to the hospital in the morning for tests."

Right around the time this was all happening, I met a passenger on the plane. It was the fourth leg of a five-leg day. I was tired and doing my usual galley routine, keeping busy, hiding out. I could hear the man before I could see him. His nylon bag brushed against the seat backs and flopped against the heads of other passengers. When he came closer, I watched him from behind the galley wall. He was old, thin, gray-haired. He plopped the bag down on the floor of the emergency-exit row. He carried a handkerchief and blotted at his mouth and nose. He had a terrible cough, my father's cough, the deep-lung kind that fades into a feathery wheeze, then just starts back up, an endless loop. A pack of Marlboros was tucked into his left sock.

I was afraid to go near him, afraid of what I might catch.

"They're not supposed to let them on like this," Brooke said.

They're not supposed to let them on drunk, either, but this was how it was.

The man coughed, then followed up with those wet-rattled breaths. I waited for Brooke to move. She didn't. She was tired, too, and not in the mood to be what our airline called "proactive." Instead of dealing with people, Brooke was alphabetizing magazines and stacking pillows in the overheads.

Whatever this man had was serious. Maybe not contagious, but serious.

"Sir, can I get you something?" I said. "Would you like some water?"

He wheezed, coughed, pointed. Coffee.

"Cream and sugar?"

He nodded, so I brought it to him, along with some water.

"Thank you," he said, and grabbed hold of my hand, the same way my father had held on to that waitress at Red Lobster. This man's hand was damp and cold. The fingers were all bone.

Later he tried to give me a tip, two quarters wrapped in a dollar, held together with a rubber band. I said no, but he pressed it into my hand.

"For taking care," he said.

The wheezing made him sound foreign, although he was an American, I'm sure, a New Yorker. The disease had taken the hardness out of his eyes. They were brown and wet. The whites were milky yellow. Like most New Yorkers, he thought small kindnesses were things you had to pay for.

But I hadn't been kind. I'd just done my job.

I took the man's money. For some reason, this made me tear up. He was dying, I was sure of it. I wondered if he was headed home, but I didn't ask. I wondered if someone would be there to meet his flight, someone who wouldn't be afraid to touch him.

"What is it they say?" the man asked me. I didn't understand. "What is it they say on TV?"

"You'll love the way we fly," Brooke singsonged from the galley.

The man nodded, then repeated the slogan, like it was something he needed to remember.

After that night in DC, I took a two-month leave and went home to help my mother take care of my father.

"It's time," she said.

In the weeks before he died, my father asked my mother to sell his Chrysler. She did, for five hundred dollars, to my uncle.

"No sense leaving it in the garage," my father said.

"Your mother, she never could drive it. Too much car for her."

People started to come by. Cousins I hadn't seen in years, neighbors, my father's stockbroker. My uncle—the one who bought the car—came every day. My father wanted to talk mostly about Sinatra, who, along with the movie critic Gene Siskel and King Hussein of Jordan, was also dying.

"That bastard Sinatra's afraid to go to sleep," my father told my uncle. "I saw it on the news. The bastard's afraid he won't wake up."

My father was afraid, too, though he wouldn't admit it.

He didn't trust the hospice nurse. He didn't want the hospital bed, the pills.

"You're trying to kill me," he told my mother. "You want me dead."

When a delivery man showed up with tanks of oxygen, my father was lying on the couch. I could see him sizing the man up. The man was young, probably in college. The job probably paid for his books.

"Let me ask you something," my father said. "How long do people live once you bring this stuff?"

The man just smiled, awkward, nervous.

"Thanks," I said. "We'll call if we have questions."

Then came the drug deliveries. The drugs were getting stronger—Ativan, morphine.

"We want him to have a good death," the nurse said. She wore Winnie-the-Pooh socks and a large crucifix around her neck. She was also a nun. "We want him to be peaceful."

Of course, there's no such thing as a good death. Simone de Beauvoir, whose grave I visited in Paris, called death an aberration. Anyone who knows death knows she was right. My father was anything but peaceful.

Before he died, my father went in and out of consciousness. My uncle was there for some of this. He was there when my father tried to open a door he saw dangling above the hospital bed. He was there when my father started to speak in Polish and wave his hands around near his mouth, little floating gestures, back and forth over his lips.

I hoped my uncle would translate the Polish for me, but he wouldn't.

"It's nonsense," he said. "He doesn't know what he's saying."

But then my uncle said something I'd never known about my father.

"What happened to the harmonica?" he asked.

One Christmas, when my father was a teenager, my grandfather, in a moment of tenderness, had gotten him a harmonica and a little songbook. My uncle said that for years, my father never went anywhere without it.

"He'd sit on the stoop and play until I wanted to pull my ears off. 'Red River Valley,' 'Oh, Susanna.' You name it, he'd play it. All day and night. He drove everyone crazy."

I'd never seen this harmonica, never heard my father even mention it, but my mother remembered it, too.

"He used to sit on the porch sometimes and just play and play," she said. "He'd sit there for hours in the dark, not talking to anybody, just him and that harmonica."

She didn't know what happened to it, and she couldn't remember when my father stopped playing. After he died, I expected to find it tucked into the pocket of an old jacket or hidden in a drawer somewhere, like the card from my mother's poor trainer.

It never showed.

I know it's not true, but now, when I think about that night my father spent with Mitch Paitch on the porch, I hear a harmonica, the smooth metal notes gliding out in the dark.

Mitch Paitch, my father had told me, was the dog in his dream. "I was the cat. He carried me. We were singing. I don't know what song," my father said.

Back in my memory, I'm in my parents' yard. I'm at my usual gruesome business, ripping the lights from the poor bugs I've caught in my jar. I crush the lights into a yellowish green paste and rub it on my arms and cheeks.

I don't think this is cruel. I think I'm Goldie Hawn in *Laugh-In. Sock it to me.* I think I am a spirit, a ghost girl. I want to be beautiful. I want my father to see me in the dark, the way I can see him, his cigarette like a small heart, keeping the beat. I run to him, crying *Can you see me? Can you see?* I want my father to sing. I want him to be happy. I want to cover us both in light.

greetings from berlin

When I began working as a flight attendant, I started a collection of postcards.

Actually, I started a wine collection first, thinking that someday I'd have a house and a cellar and a glorious bottle of very rare 1994 French Merlot to crack open before dinner, but I kept drinking it up.

I still have the postcards, though, bags of them. And I know, whenever I sort through them, that I was hungover and sick in New Orleans; that I was lonely and binge-popping chocolates shaped like chubby mushrooms in Brussels; that I stayed in bed for twenty-four hours in Vegas, the neon lights of the Strip pulsing like monitored heartbeats off the hotel room walls.

Whenever I shuffle those beautiful cards, I think of Frank O'Hara, that sweet tragic man, and his poems, and that he himself sold postcards at the Museum of Modern Art in New York, where he'd run back and forth between his cash register and an old typewriter he'd keep at the far end of the counter, writing poems on the fly.

Before my father was diagnosed with the cancer that

would kill him, he and my mother came along on a trip I was working. A Sheldon special—New York to Berlin. A twenty-four-hour layover.

Because of their parents-of-an-employee flight privileges, my parents were flying free in Business Class. I was working up there with two senior German flight attendants, Helga and Dana, who had a long and tumultuous history. Apparently once, about ten years before, one of them told the other to go fuck herself. And so, throughout the flight, they worked hard to make each other insane.

Helga would set up a coffee service. Dana would tear it down and redo it for tea. Helga would slice the lemons lengthwise. Dana would take the wedges and cut them into chunks, then spear them with toothpicks she'd take from the bathroom.

This went on for the first three hours until finally a fistfight, complete with the sound of shattering glass, broke out in the galley. The captain had to come back and break it up. Helga was sent to work in Coach, and I was left alone with Dana, who was, in addition to being German and very serious, a terrible snob.

Mealtime came, and my parents ordered prime rib, which, like most food on an airplane, is pretty terrifying. The slab of meat comes out like a bull's-eye, the unnatural circles of chemically engineered pink and red flesh stare up from the plate. And so I wasn't surprised that, when Dana brought my parents their meals, they sent them back, asking to have them cooked through.

This made Dana furious.

"Don't they know," she said, her accent enhancing each syllable with a bit of spit, "that it's supposed to bleed a little?"

Here's the worst part. Looking back, I know Dana was awful, but I cared what she thought of my parents, of my family, of me. I wanted to impress. I wanted to show that I, too, was worldly and wise in the ways of travel and meat.

In that moment with Dana, a Berliner who believed that, with the Jews off limits, gypsies were now responsible for all the evil in the world, I felt like Andy Warhol.

One of Warhol's Marilyns still puckers up on a wall in the front office at Warhola Scrap Metals, a junkyard that the artist's family still owns and operates in Carrick, near Pittsburgh's South Side.

When Warhol moved to New York to become an artist, he dropped the *a* from his last name and told interviewers that he was born on the Lower East Side. I always thought it was horrible the way he was embarrassed about his native land, his working-class history, his Old World family.

But there, on that plane with that horrible woman, I was embarrassed—of my parents, of my father's green polyester suit and too-wide tie, of my mother's Aqua Net hairdo, of how awkward and out of place they were, there in Business Class, *traveling in luxury like the rich*, of my father, turning to the impeccable German businessman next to him and shouting, one syllable at a time—"Do You Speak A-Mer-I-Can?"

What did I know?

When he was very sick, my father would talk about that trip, the wonderful airplane food, the good service, how proud I made him because he watched me being kind to other passengers.

As for Berlin itself, he was lavish with praise—the most glorious city in the world; the streets so clean they sparkled like bits of glass were embedded in the asphalt; and no parking meters—you could park anywhere, the sign of true civilization. But most of all, the air was clean.

"I can really breathe in Berlin," my father would say.

As Sheldon knew, I always hated Germany, and I always thought my father, as a World War II veteran, would feel the same way. What I remember about that city is the bombed-out church, and the fresh coat of Nazi graffiti all around its base. But for my father what mattered is that we were all there, together, the three of us. What mattered was that the Berlin Wall was down—a miracle in my father's lifetime—and that the strudel at the café across from our hotel was hot and they gave it to you wrapped in waxed paper so that you could eat it right away. The coffee at the Berlin McDonald's was fresh and dark and nearly everyone was beautiful and blond and spoke English.

Now, years after my father's death, I keep a picture of him in my living room. This one's from another trip, to Rome. I wasn't there, and so it was my mother behind the camera. My father is standing next to a young man with very thick eyebrows and an acoustic guitar. My father is in profile—all of his attention is on the man, his music. I wasn't there, but my mother says my father—who back home wouldn't even listen to music, who Scotch-taped the dial of his old transistor radio to KQV-AM All-Talk All-The-Time so he'd never lose the station—is singing along.

She doesn't remember which song, but I like to think it's "Spanish Eyes," one of my father's old favorites from his Braddock days, and a likely one, since this restaurant is near the Spanish Steps and the song is a staple among Italian street musicians.

In family pictures, my father always scowled for the camera, a cigarette dangling James-Dean-like from the corner of his downturned mouth. But in this picture, the pack of Pall Malls bulges in his shirt pocket and my father is smiling. He's performing to a crowd. The tops of their heads fill the foreground, and off to the left, a beautiful dark-haired woman is laughing and clapping for my father, in Italy, in this good restaurant, singing.

On the postcard my parents sent me from Rome, there's a picture of the Trevi Fountain at night, with Neptune and his horses all lit up and golden.

"Three coins in a fountain," my mother wrote in her practiced flowery scrawl. "We made wishes."

"Pennies," my father printed underneath. "Wish you were here."

the hotel amigo,
the hotel ideal

Just over a year before my father died, my parents and I spent a week together in Paris. We were getting the most out of the flight privileges that were the benefits of my job. My parents, who once said the French were snottier than poodles, loved Paris. We had rooms at the Hotel Ideal, a matchstick of a building on Avenue Emile Zola, near the Eiffel Tower.

The Hotel Ideal has small pink rooms stuffed full of the basics—single beds, nightstands, a bathroom. My room was on the sixth floor. It had tall pink-shuttered windows that opened out. I had a view of the rooftops of Paris, and woke to the sound of pigeons cooing every morning. For breakfast, the Hotel Ideal served coffee and warm croissants in a basement dining room. Down the street was a grocery store where I could buy wine and cheese and bread for about five dollars.

The Hotel Ideal is, I suppose, a dive by most standards. The guidebooks give it two stars, one step up from a hostel. I thought it was the most perfect place in the world.

I have a picture of my father and me standing outside the hotel. His arm is tight around my shoulder and he's grinning. My father rarely grinned, but there he is. In the picture, he looks shorter than I remember him. Neither of us knew he was already sick, that the cancer had already begun to spread. We were in Paris. It was springtime. These were lines from songs he used to sing when he was young.

When Jacques Brel first settled in Paris, he stayed at the Hotel Ideal. Neither my parents nor I knew this at the time, and I suppose it wouldn't have meant much. Brel wouldn't have liked us there. He didn't think much of Americans, hated the Vietnam War, and refused to sing or write in English. He died in Bobigny, a suburb of Paris, in 1978, of lung cancer, like my father, and is buried on Hiva Oa in the Marquesas Islands. His grave is a few yards away from Gauguin's.

It was the Parisian talent scout Paul Canetti who first invited Brel to try Paris and launched Brel's life as "a man who belonged to no one, except, perhaps, his public." This has become the motto of the Jacques Brel Foundation, even though, when he was alive, Brel was married, with three daughters and many mistresses.

According to the foundation, Jacques Brel was alive and well in all who loved him. When he died, the foundation says, "he took with him a little of the potential that lies dormant in each of our hearts."

The first trip I worked after my father's death was Brussels, a forty-eight-hour layover at the Hotel Amigo, just off Brussels's Grand Place. When I stood in the lobby,

I remembered Becky, the human metronome, and Tish with her ridiculous props at the Trafford talent show, and how important Brel had been to us all. There at the Amigo's front desk, I picked up a brochure for "The Jacques Brel Lovers' Package," and I knew I was home.

I hadn't been to Brussels before, and so I decided to take in the sights with a pilot who was, of course, a history buff. Most pilots are history buffs and/or Tom Clancy fans, and I usually don't get cornered alone with one of them. But this time, I was sad and lonely and didn't feel up to exploring the city on my own, not even the Brel exhibit, so I made an exception.

The pilot was marginally cute in that Top Gun kind of way, even when he lectured about Belgian history and whined about his lousy marriage—pilot-ese for "Life is short and unhappy. Let's have sex." (I didn't.)

Still, we did get to visit the cafés that Jacques Berel, The Eccentric, loved so much. We ate mussels soaked in garlic and wine. We drank lots of good Belgian beer. We visited the famous statues of Manneken Pis and his sister, both peeing cheerily in their fountains. By the end of the night, I felt lighter and glad for the company.

On the way back to the hotel, we stopped at another statue tucked between chocolate shops off the Grand Place. The statue, bronze and serious, is of T'Serclaes, the "liberator of Brussels," who was murdered in 1386.

T'Serclaes is in agony. His attackers have cut out his tongue. They have amputated his left foot. His neck muscles are tight as violin strings.

"It's good luck to touch it," the pilot said, and I saw how the statue shined in intimate places, the bowls of T'Serclaes's cheeks, the notch above his right knee, the delicate wishbones of his one remaining foot, all the places strangers have rubbed, this time for money, this time for love.

Jacques Brel's life belonged to no one, except, maybe, his public.

And I couldn't help it. I was thinking of my father, and those thirty-six cars in his funeral procession.

"Thirty-six cars," my mother said, having counted them herself. "Imagine."

My father, in death, was suddenly popular.

The little funeral home in Trafford was overrun with lost family and friends, who lined up to kneel at his coffin, touch his hands, his face, smooth the lapels of his one good suit, even kiss the silver crucifix that dangled from the rosary between his fingers.

Before he died, Jacques Brel made several final appearances at his favorite venues in Paris and Brussels. The posters read, JACQUES BREL SAYS GOOD-BYE. There are photos of him onstage, accepting roses and reaching down to touch the crowds. And then he put on his sailing cap, the traditional striped shirt, and sailed across the Pacific in his yacht.

I don't know if any of those people at the funeral home touched my father when he was alive, or whether it was grief or something else that propelled them. I didn't know many of them, or what their presence there might have meant. Mostly I just stood by the casket or next to the bulletin board where the funeral director had pinned pictures of my father.

My mother and I had collected the pictures at the funeral director's request.

"It's a new tradition," he'd told us. "A celebration of life in death. People really like it."

My mother and I pulled stacks of decaying shoe boxes from her closet. We went through hundreds of pictures. We chose one with my father puffing on a cigarette, his trademark filterless Pall Mall, with the mountains of Switzerland behind him. We chose one of him in uniform on his aircraft carrier, the *Lexington*. We picked a wedding picture, a family Christmas picture, and a picture of my parents at a Florida beach when they were young.

In that last picture, my mother is in a two-piece bathing suit. She didn't want to use the picture because of this, thinking it wouldn't be proper to be seen half naked and joyful in a funeral home, but I convinced her. Her bathing suit top laces up, and my mother is as curvy and beautiful as a dark-haired Marilyn Monroe. She's wearing a floppy sun hat and ankle-wrap espadrilles. My father is tan and movie-star handsome himself in madras plaid swim trunks. His right arm is around my mother's shoulder, his left hand wrapped around a bottle of beer.

As long as I knew him, my father never wore jewelry, not even his wedding ring, citing occupational hazards, the machines that ground steel into dust.

"That's how guys lose a finger," he said.

But here, on this beach in 1961, my father is wearing a signet ring on his left pinkie.

"Oh that," my mother said. "Your father, he liked to dress."

I don't know what happened to the ring, although I saw it in one other picture, this one of my parents at The White Elephant, an old nightclub in White Oak, where they'd gone to hear Mitch Miller, and Swing and Sway with Sammy Kaye.

On the table in front of them are drinks, whiskey sours probably, a cherry bobbing in each one. My mother is wearing a pearl brooch and a little hat with netting that falls just above her eyebrows. My father is in a pin-striped suit and his thick black hair is combed into waves. And there's his hand, the fingernails clipped and clean, and that ring, dangling over my mother's left shoulder.

They could have been a famous couple, smiling for the paparazzi who caught them in a private moment, there, at the smoky White Elephant, where music filled up the darkness and everyone was beautiful.

new york is a city of bridges

After my father died, my mother, who'd never been very healthy, became very ill. A bad heart and bad nerves, not to mention loneliness, were only the start of it. And so the airline gave me another leave—this one for five years—to go back to Pittsburgh to take care of her.

I'd already gotten an apartment and another job back home—this time teaching writing at a university. It would have been my dream job if it had been in New York.

A year later, at this job, I'd meet my husband, who'd grown up in Irwin, about six miles from my hometown. We'd fall in love over big fish sandwiches and beers at a bar called The Squirrel Cage. Within five years, we'd have a son and a daughter. We'd be happy.

But I didn't know any of this. Back then, all I knew was, I loved my mother, I worried for her, I wanted to be a good daughter, and, since I didn't have any brothers or sisters and my mother's siblings weren't much help, I didn't have a choice.

What I'd never say was, I thought my life was over.

Even though on all practical counts I was ready to go and I didn't have many things to pack, it took me a week to finally decide on a day to leave.

"Tomorrow," I told my mother.

"What time exactly?" she said.

"If traffic works out, I should be there by six," I said.

"So late," she said.

I figured I'd leave around 11 AM, take the Triboro to the George Washington so that I could look at the city one more time, and make it to Pittsburgh in about seven hours. That meant I could stay up late, pace around my apartment, drink the bottle of wine I'd brought from my last trip to Madrid, do some last-minute packing, and sleep in until ten.

At seven the next morning, I woke up, wine headache intact, to the sound of a chain saw.

You'd think that since we are talking New York—Kew Gardens, Queens, to be exact—and not the woodlands of Oregon or a horror-movie set somewhere in Texas, this would have been alarming. But as with most things that happened in my neighborhood, I was used to it. This apartment—finally my own small, rent-controlled place— was just blocks from where I'd lived when I first moved to New York, back when I had eight roommates. I'd had this place for almost a year, and hated to give it up, even if the neighborhood and neighbors weren't ideal.

For instance—the chain saw.

When I told my mother "tomorrow," I'd forgotten that

tomorrow meant Wednesday. Every Wednesday, around 7 AM, Rocco, my neighbor three floors up, would be down on the sidewalk, cutting up scrap metal to sell at the junk-yards and chopshops in Flushing.

Every Tuesday, he'd rummage through the trash that piled up in Dumpsters, the basement, and along the street outside of our brown tenement building. He'd fill a shop-ping cart—lifted from Associated Foods a few blocks over—with copper wire, busted air conditioners, banged-up pots and pans, washing-machine lids, and hubcaps. Wednesday mornings, he'd break out the chain saw and cut it all into sellable chunks.

When the chain saw revved up, nobody in the neigh-borhood called the police. Like me, mostly they'd grown used to it. They called him Mungo Rocco, like Mungo Jerry, the 1970s Top-of-the-Pops skiffle-jug band, or bet-ter, like Mungo Jerry's namesake, Mungojerrie, a junkyard cat from T. S. Eliot's *Old Possum's Book of Practical Cats*.

When it came to Rocco, the Eliot reference—a raggedy but wise pack rat of a cat—made the most sense, although in the neighborhood, people pronounced *Mungo* like *Mongo*, which made Rocco either a mongoose or Mongolian currency.

Both of those worked, too.

"I got a head for numbers," Rocco said. "Everything's money to me."

On my last Wednesday in New York, the chain saw was giving Rocco trouble. I could hear him swearing and kicking at what sounded like a disembodied car fender.

"Motherfucker piece of shit. Come on already."

The chain saw kicked up again and the sound was like a drill stabbing at a giant molar and amplified through the loudspeakers at Giants Stadium.

I pulled the covers and a pillow over my head.

From underneath the pillow, I yelled, "Knock it off already, for fuck's sake."

I slammed my fists into the mattress. Then I got up and took a shower.

According to Jake, our on-the-take super, the story goes like this:

Rocco was a genius back at Richmond Hill High School. He was also huge and violent, a street brawler who stood out even at a school where students occasionally threw one another off the roof and where once a student came to class with a sawed-off pitchfork and speared a poor math teacher in the back.

The story is, Rocco was recruited young and went off to break legs for the Gotti family. He'd show up at school with a Rolex, good shoes, a wad of hundreds held together by a gold money clip. When he graduated from high school, he owned two apartment buildings.

The story is, with the money came drugs, and Rocco got a taste for heroin. The Gotti family didn't like Rocco's habit—not to mention his weight loss—and so he was dismissed.

Soon Rocco traded his designer suits for do-rags and flannel shirts and started his own businesses on the side—mostly credit-card theft, mail theft, fake IDs, and making deliveries of whatever anyone wanted to pay him to deliver. He was doing okay until he was busted by the cops, did time on Rikers (a time Rocco himself refers to as "Not bad—three hots and a cot"), got hooked on methadone, got out, moved in with his mother, bought her a big-screen TV with money he'd saved up from his Gotti days, fell in love with another methadone addict who went back to heroin and died, and ended up what people in the neighborhood called an EDP—New-York-cop lingo for Emotionally Disturbed Person.

Who knows.

If I hadn't heard anything, based on my own experience—aside from the time he decided to do some target practice with a sniper rifle in the laundry room, and aside from the time he asked me to help him make business cards with only his beeper number on them, and aside from his perpetual chainsawing—I'd say Rocco was pretty ordinary.

Mostly, we said hello.

Sometimes just a nod.

When he'd see me in my uniform, headed to work, he'd say, "Hey, fly girl, have a good trip."

Sometimes I was surprised when I came home and nobody had broken into my apartment.

Whenever I went to Europe, I'd bring back chocolate bars and give Rocco a few. I didn't know then that methadone addicts aren't supposed to have chocolate bars, or that that's why Rocco was so happy to have them. But still.

Once, when he saw me carrying some books, he wanted to talk about Salman Rushdie and *The Satanic Verses.*

"I read that one," he said, looking off over my shoulder, the way most people in that neighborhood did in casual conversation. Looking straight into someone else's eyes was reserved for when you meant business, whatever business you were in at the moment.

"I don't see the big deal," he said. "Even Cat Stevens wants this guy dead, right? Mr. Peace Train and all that? All that hippie-doo-dah, and now he wants to kill this guy? For what? That's some fucked-up shit."

"I know, right," I said.

That was pretty much our longest conversation ever.

The chain saw was really going at something big— probably the car fender—by the time I was out of the shower. I pulled on some sweats and started carrying a few last boxes to my car, an old white Ford that had belonged to my father. Since it had been with me in New York, the front and rear bumpers were full of dents and the side door was scratched and kicked in. My father would have hated that.

"Hey, Pittsburgh," Rocco said, and he let the chain saw go down to a putter, then stall.

A lot of people in my neighborhood called me Pittsburgh. I think it translated to hillbilly or sucker.

"Hey, Pittsburgh, where you going?"

"Home," I said. "My mother's sick."

"You gotta take care of your mother," he said.

Rocco's mother, I knew, had been sick for a while. I

think she had chemo, because she was almost bald and rarely went out without a bandanna wrapped around her head. She looked a little crazy, too, walking around the neighborhood in a faded housedress and ripped-up Keds, muttering to herself.

The last time the police came for Rocco—Jake called them about the sniper-rifle incident—they broke her front door and one of the cops put a billy club through the big-screen TV Rocco had bought her.

When I left New York, Rocco was out on bail, threatening to sue the police department for excessive use of force, and saving up for a new TV.

"My mother," he said. "She likes her soaps."

"You want to check and see if I've got anything left you can use?" I asked him.

"Everything's money to me," he said, and followed me up to my nearly empty rooms.

"You taking that air conditioner?" he asked.

I shook my head. "It doesn't work."

"Okay then."

He took the air conditioner, the broken stereo I'd been using as a plant stand, a box fan, and a couple of old pasta pots.

"Good luck," he said.

"You, too," I said.

Later, when I finally drove off, Rocco was still there on the sidewalk with his chain saw. He was about to go to work on the air conditioner. He lifted one hand—not a wave really, just one hand up in the air—and I honked back.

This is what it came down to—Rocco in my rearview mirror; the rambling worn-down apartment complex we shared; the cars parked bumper-to-bumper on Curzon, a street with a name so close to the Spanish word *corazon*, for "heart"; the kind little Korean woman arranging bouquets of calla lilies outside her grocery on Metropolitan Avenue; the huge shamrock on the KARAOKE TONIGHT sign on Yer Man's Pub. This was my New York, full of small moments that had little to do with the glamorous city I'd imagined years ago.

Once, when describing a cab ride he was taking down Park Avenue in winter, F. Scott Fitzgerald wrote that he knew he would never be so happy again. By the time I got to the George Washington Bridge, I felt the same way.

Of all of Jake's stories about Rocco, there's one I know is true. He did have a girlfriend. Her name was Lucia.

Once, stuck together in the rickety elevator in our building, I noticed what looked like the edges of a new tattoo sticking out from the sleeve of Rocco's T-shirt. The skin was red and swollen, and tiny scabs had formed around the bottom edges of what looked like a huge rose on his right bicep.

"New tattoo?" I said. "Looks like it hurt."

He pulled up his sleeve.

The rose was the size of a fist. Huge drops of water fell from the petals, which drooped from a thick thorny stem. In one of the drops were the words LUCIA 4EVER.

"My girlfriend. She died," he said.

"I'm sorry," I said.

"She used to listen to me," he said.

After my father died, my mother said she missed having someone to talk to when she couldn't sleep.

"The house is too quiet," she'd say.

My coming home didn't completely change that. And even though she'd live almost five years after he died, there was never much I could do about my mother's loneliness. She missed my father, his body there on the couch in front of the TV, there on the right side of the bed, in his chair at the kitchen table. She missed the small things he did— cleaning the furnace, changing the car's oil, tightening screws, opening jars when the lids were screwed on too tight.

I miss my father, too. I'm just now starting to dream about him, and that seems to help some. Mostly, I dream about him driving his old Chrysler. I'm a girl again, and we're on our way to Florida. I'm looking at my father from the back. His hair is thick and black, no sign of cancer. He's smoking a cigarette and flicking the ashes out of the open window. He says, "How you doing back there?" I don't remember whether I answer him in my dream or not.

I dream about New York, too, all the time. When I do, the city is still whole, and I'm grateful for that. Everything is the way it was when I left it back in 2000.

In my dreams, it's almost always night. The towers are still standing. There are lights in the windows and people are in there, working late. Down in New York Bay, there are swarms of ferries filled with people who just want to look at the city.

Sometimes I'm back in a café, maybe Café Tina or Café Vittorio. Sometimes Vittorio's there, making amends over losing his temper with yet another customer who would not pay. Vittorio's smoothing his good suit and saying, "I do not know what came over me." He offers his home-made tiramisu, the creamiest, most delicious thing I've ever tasted.

Sometimes I dream I'm back in Queens and Rocco is there, on the stoop outside the building or down on the sidewalk, grinding away at a stubborn broken-down washer. His mother, I know, is inside their apartment watching *As the World Turns* or *One Life to Live*.

Sometimes, when I dream like this, I do what I did when I was flying. I wake up and am not sure where I am. So much of Pittsburgh looks like a shrunken-down version of New York that sometimes I have trouble in the daytime, too. Pittsburgh's South Side becomes the East Village. Squirrel Hill becomes Kew Gardens. And of course, the Andy Warhol museum is here, in Pittsburgh. Explain that.

Now that I'm back, living in the same house I grew up in, I still romanticize New York too much. Despite every-thing that happened to me there, despite how my life changed during those years, I still love it more than any other place on earth. I don't care how that sounds. I love it, I suppose, unnaturally, the way you're supposed to love another person.

I have to catch myself again and again. I don't want to be one of those people who always has to say how things are better someplace else. We Pittsburghers are proud people, too. And, as my friend Bob Pajich would say, we don't need no uppity New Yorker telling us how to live.

And so, there you have it.

Back when I was flying, sometimes I'd work the lazy girl's late-night shuffle. It was an easy shuttle rotation, DC to New York. I didn't do it for the money, really. There wasn't a lot of flight time, so the trip wasn't worth much. But the last leg would get into New York around 11 PM and the flight would be nearly empty, which meant it was peaceful.

On our approach into LaGuardia, I'd plop down into a passenger seat and watch as we floated above the whole city. From where I sat, it looked more like the model of a city, one that had been lit up for Christmas.

Ghislain and I were both wrong about Paris, after all. From the air, New York was and still is the most beautiful thing I've ever seen.

On those late-night flights, the plane would come in low. The lights of the city were so bright, it hurt to look at them from inside the dark cabin. But I looked, and from up there, I could see all the traffic on all the bridges. I've never been good at geography, but I'd come to know the city by heart and so I could name all of them—the Queensboro, Triboro, George Washington, Manhattan, and, of course, the Brooklyn. I could estimate just how long my commute would take based on where the taillights backed up on the Grand Central.

From all the way up there, I could map my way home.

about the author

LORI JAKIELA: I am both vain and nearsighted. I don't like to wear glasses, even the hipster ones I bought in grad school to make me look like a serious artist.

I think *slippy* should be a real word because it sounds so much slippier than *slippery*.

Jakiela rhymes with *tequila*, and, because I'm a native Pittsburgher and prone to all sorts of odd and gritty sentiments, I occasionally drink Iron City Beer. If you've never had an Iron City Beer, suck on your car keys. You'll get the idea.

Sometimes, maybe for all of the above reasons, I see things. Seeing things is not a particularly good trait for a memoirist to have, but there you go.

Back in high school, when I'd rather reveal my bra size than put on a pair of glasses, I'd scrunch up my face until my eyes looked like two coin slots. Still, I could barely make out the writing on the blackboard. This may be why I had such a hard time in math class, where all the ones looked like fours, and why, for a while, I saw cows. Everywhere. Holsteins, to be precise.

But I digress.

And so at first I thought my brain was misfiring the day I crossed Pittsburgh's Liberty Bridge and saw signs for the Brooklyn Bridge where signs for the Strip District should have been.

But the signs were real.

Although I didn't know it at the time, a movie crew was in town. They were shooting, as they often did, some film that was supposed to be set in New York. This was a few years back, and it was cheaper to film in Pittsburgh then. On screen, it was almost impossible to tell the two cities, with their filthy rivers and Fifth Avenues, apart.

I still think about that moment as a metaphor, for my life, sure, and, now, for the book you're holding. This is a book about those two cities—New York and Pittsburgh. It's also a book about two dreams: my own, sprouted while watching *That Girl* reruns on a console TV with jiggly rabbit ears; and my father's—the dreams of a steelworker who wanted to sing on Broadway. It's a book about how things converge—cities, dreams, lives. And it's a book about running from and coming home, cows or no cows.

More than any of that, I hope it's a book that has, maybe in spite of me, a bit of grace in it. The poet Ed Ochester once told me that grace is the ability to be loving or joking or caring in the face of the knowledge that human beings will die, that we're all likely to have some big troubles in our lives.

"Essentially," he said, "in the face of that knowledge, to be able to celebrate life."

And so, here's to the dreamers—nearsighted, farsighted, New York, Pittsburgh, wherever you land.

Visit my Web site at www.lorijakiela.com.

Lori Jakiela

some great books
and authors

Changing the Name to Ochester and *The Land of Cockaigne*, by Ed Ochester

The Honeymooners and *The Last Mountain Dancer*, by Chuck Kinder

Stand Up, Friend, With Me, by Ed Field

Anagrams, by Lorrie Moore

Dress Your Family in Corduroy and Denim, by David Sedaris

What's Not to Love and *Wake Up, Sir*, by Jonathan Ames

Lunch Poems, by Frank O'Hara

The Branch Will Not Break, by James Wright

The Hospital Poems, by Gerald Locklin

Punch, by Dave Newman

Places, Everyone, by Jim Daniels

The Brotherhood of the Grape, by John Fante

Everyone, Exquisite, by Bob Pajich

Star-Spangled Banner, by Denise Duhamel

Swimming Sweet Arrow, by Maureen Gibbon

The Door Open to the Fire, by Judith Vollmer

Human Landscapes, by Nazim Hikmet

Mad River, by Jan Beatty

The Lemon, by Mohammed Mrabet

Post Office, by Charles Bukowski

Angelhead, by Greg Bottoms

The Accidental Buddhist, by Dinty Moore

five insights from a world traveler

In many countries, the traditional American sign for "okay"—forefinger and thumb touching to make a circle, other three fingers straight up—means "okay, screw you." Use sparingly, only when you mean it, and never in Turkey. **1**

2 Around the world, the two most recognizable words are *Coke* and *okay*. Although most people can handle *Coke* and *okay*, those who do not speak English will not suddenly understand English, no matter how loudly or slowly you speak it.

3 Security tip: Vibrators look suspicious during a luggage scan. If caught with one, you'll have to take it out of your suitcase, remove and replace the batteries, and demonstrate that it does, in fact, vibrate.

Flight attendants—flammable polyester uniforms and cute little wings aside—are not parts of airplanes. Therefore, do not grope, poke, or attempt to stow a flight attendant without his or her permission.

5 When handed a pack of peanuts on a flight, it is neither funny nor acceptable to say, "No thanks, I'll have the lobster."